Writing Workshop
in Middle School

What You Need to *Really* Make It Work— in the Time You've Got

Marilyn Pryle

■ **SCHOLASTIC**

New York • Toronto • London • Auckland • Sydney
Mexico City • New Delhi • Hong Kong • Buenos Aires

Dedication

For my students, past, present and future, who inspire me and teach me,
and who embody the goodness and potential of this world.

Acknowledgments

I am deeply grateful for the support of many people. Ann Keenan, Michael Connelly, and Mary Cunningham of the Braintree Schools first gave me the chance to create my own writing workshop in Braintree, Massachusetts. My guides along the way include fellow teachers Dave Wilson, Dr. Bonnie Alco, and Dr. Jeff Cantrell, and Nancie Atwell, without whose book *In the Middle* I would not have known where to start. I am also grateful to the Abington Heights School District in Clarks Summit, Pennsylvania, for their continued support of my work. Of course, this book would not exist without the encouragement, vision, and hard work of many people at Scholastic, including Virginia Dooley, Joanna Davis-Swing, and Sarah Glasscock, and I thank them sincerely. Finally, I am grateful for the support of my friends and family, especially my parents Ernest and Patricia Bogusch, my husband Tim, and my sons Gavin and Tiernan.

• ● ●

Cover designer: Jorge J. Namerow
Cover photograph: © Grady Reese/IStock
Interior design: Sarah Morrow
Development Editor: Joanna Davis-Swing
Editor: Sarah Glasscock

ISBN: 978-0-545-28070-9
Copyright © 2012 by Marilyn Pryle
All rights reserved.
Printed in the U.S.A.

1 2 3 4 5 6 7 8 9 10   40   19 18 17 16 15 14 13

Contents

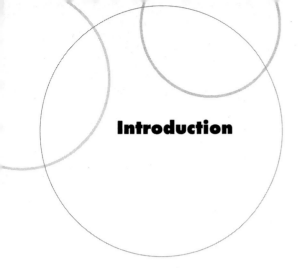

Introduction

I strode down the long, patterned halls of the convention center, wheeling my rolling backpack behind me. I was scheduled to present "Writing Workshop: Where Do I Start?" 30 minutes later. I had scoped out the room the day before, so I felt prepared. The space could hold 70 people, which was larger than the other rooms where I'd spoken over the past few years at various conferences. Usually about a dozen participants showed up; anything beyond that I considered outstanding (once I had about 20). I'll just have this group sit in the front half of the room, I thought, as I reached the assigned door and pushed it open.

I stopped, palm on door. In the seats, roughly 10 people were already scattered, flipping through their programs, taking notes, or just relaxing. Did I have the wrong room? Was someone else finishing up? I looked to the front: empty. I proceeded to the podium, smiled cautiously at the early birds (maybe they didn't yet realize they were in the wrong place), and checked my program. I was in the right room, 30 minutes early, just as I'd planned.

"Is this the room for writing workshop?" asked a young man, leaning in the door.

"Yes, come on in," I replied, growing exuberant.

Twenty minutes later, the room was full. I asked people to scoot toward the center of their rows; I moved the presenters' chairs into the aisles and put my coat and bags on the floor. Still people came. They dragged in chairs from the hallway and, finally, sat on the floor along the sides of the room. I could hardly breathe when I realized how many people were in the room.

I knew they were not there for me; I was one of dozens and dozens of educators sharing their expertise and experience. The participants in that room were there for writing workshop. They were there because they either knew the subject firsthand or were curious about the benefits of a writing workshop. Maybe they were unsatisfied with the results they'd gained from packaged writing prompts, or maybe some were writers themselves, who knew that teaching writing had to be more organic and genuine than the methods prescribed in textbooks. They came because they already believed in, or had a hunch about, the power of having their students write real, personal, self-selected pieces in a setting that focuses on process, individual attention, and personal growth.

Writing Workshop in Middle School © 2013 by Marilyn Pryle • Scholastic

But the attendees came for even more than that: the workshop was titled not just "Writing Workshop" but "Writing Workshop: Where Do I Start?" The people in that room presumably felt overwhelmed, or at least confused, by the idea of beginning a writing workshop. We can read about the theory of writing workshop all we want, agreeing enthusiastically with its principles, but when it is time to face the 25 eager beings sitting before us in the classroom, pedagogy falters. We wonder how we can possibly manage it. How can we model, read, instruct, suggest, discuss, assign, and grade all of it in a way that encourages each student individually? The 90 or so people in that room sought answers to these questions.

I have written other books about writing workshop, each focusing on some specific angle: assignments, conferencing, test taking, and so on. My goal in this book is to backtrack, to go to the very beginning and explain in detail my experience with setting up and running a writing workshop. I want no teacher to ever be intimidated or queasy about the thought of writing workshop; on the contrary, I want teachers who are inclined toward a workshop to feel enthusiastic about its possibilities. Above all, I want all readers to believe that, *with organization, anything is possible.*

Because I have tried to incorporate all components of writing workshop here, I have drawn from each of my previous books in writing this one. Readers of those books will find pockets of familiar discussion. I include a list of the other books on the next page, as they fully explain certain topics that can only be introduced here due to space constraints. I encourage readers drawn to these topics to pursue them in my earlier books and any other books you can find. The more confident you feel about writing workshop, the more comfortable your students will feel, the more willing they will be to take risks and put their true minds and hearts on paper.

Let us begin, then, at the beginning. Let us find the way to entice our students to open up, to express themselves genuinely, to work on their words and minds like clay—molding and remolding. Let us give them the tools they can use long after they leave our classes, the confidence that will serve them for life. Let us show them that their thoughts are important, that they have something to say, that becoming a better writer makes them better thinkers, better livers of life.

How To Use This Book

This book is structured to take readers through the process of setting up and running a writing workshop. The first chapters deal with the philosophy of writing workshop and how to create an overall plan for a semester or year. The middle chapters give practical suggestions about starting and pacing a workshop, grading, and individual conferencing. The book ends with ideas about incorporating standardized test practice into a workshop and adapting a workshop to support a literature class or an ELL class. To reap the full benefits of this material, first read the book in its entirety; this will make it a much more fruitful reference for you.

Note: *Throughout this book I have included "Student Notes"—snippets of students' own thoughts taken from surveys I give midyear and at the end of the year.*

My previous books offer more in-depth discussion of the following material in this book:

- *Teaching Students to Write Effective Essays: Meaningful, Step-by-Step Lessons That Get Students Ready for Writing Assessments.* Many of the genre assignments are explained fully in this book, including the following: Introductory Letter, Process Essay, Compare-and-Contrast Essay, Short Story Analysis, and Analysis of a Poem. Each assignment is differentiated and has two sample readings, prewriting pages, assignment sheets with rubrics, and three mini-lessons.

- *Purposeful Conferences: Powerful Writing! Strategies, Tips, and Teacher-Student Dialogues That Really Help Kids Improve Their Writing.* All aspects of conferencing with students are discussed in this book. It fully develops the topics in Chapter 8.

- *Easy & Effective Writing Lessons for English Language Learners: Scaffolded Assignments That Help ELLs Succeed in the Mainstream Classroom.* Here is a sampling of the assignments in this book: Setting Sketch, Character Sketch, Ode, Autobiographical Incident, Travel Brochure, and Letter to the Principal. This book expands on the material in Chapter 10.

Bibliography

2013 Poet's Market. (2013). Blue Ash, OH: Writer's Digest Books.

2013 Writer's Market. (2013). Blue Ash, OH: Writer's Digest Books.

Atwell, N. (1998). *In the middle: New understandings about writing, reading, and learning.* Portsmouth, NH: Boynton/Cook Publishers.

Heard, G. (1995). *Writing toward home: Tales and lessons to find your way.* Portsmouth, NH: Heinemann.

Murray, D. (1990). *Shoptalk: Learning to write with writers.* Portsmouth, NH: Boynton/Cook.

Pryle, M. (2007). *Teaching students to write effective essays: Meaningful, step-by-step lessons that get students ready for writing assessments.* New York: Scholastic.

Pryle, M. (2009). *Purposeful conferences: Powerful writing! Strategies, tips, and teacher-student dialogues that really help kids improve their writing.* New York: Scholastic.

Pryle, M. (2010). *Easy & effective writing lessons for English language learners: Scaffolded assignments that help ELLs succeed in the mainstream classroom.* New York: Scholastic.

Watcyn-Jones, P., & Howard-Williams, D. (2004). *Pair Work 1: Elementary-Intermediate* (2nd ed.). White Plains, NY: Pearson ESL.

Watcyn-Jones, P. (2003). *Pair Work 2: Intermediate-Upper Intermediate.* White Plains, NY: Pearson ESL.

Watcyn-Jones, P., & Howard-Williams, D. (2004). *Pair Work 3: Upper Intermediate-Advanced.* White Plains, NY: Pearson ESL.

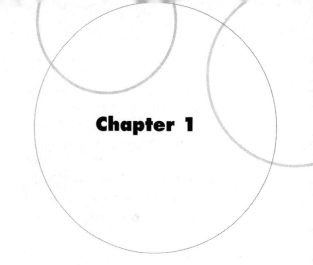

Chapter 1

The Pillars of Writing Workshop: Authenticity and Choice

What is writing workshop? What is the difference between learning writing in a workshop and learning writing in a more formal class setting? *Is* there a difference, and is it for the better?

A "writing class" usually comprises a one-size-fits-all instruction and blanket assignments for all. A workshop, however, is individualized, accommodating each student's needs and interests.

Every teacher knows the stages of the writing process: prewriting, drafting, revising, and editing. We introduce these stages to students; we hang posters listing them on our walls. But how, if we simply assign topics or prompts and grade student papers without letting them revise afterward, is this process being demonstrated or reinforced? A typical writing class focuses on the finished product: an assignment is given, students complete it outside of class (at home, presumably), the finished product is returned, and grades are levied. Not so in a workshop: the focus here is on process, on development, on revising, and on revising again. The process *is* the workshop.

In a regular class in which writing is simply assigned, graded, and returned, students are left to guess at what the teacher's corrections and suggestions may mean. And, as all teachers know, most students rarely even *read* the comments we laboriously etch late at night; they flip to the grade and stuff the paper in a folder. As a result, they often remain stagnant in their writing growth, repeatedly making the same basic mistakes. In a workshop, though, a teacher can meet with students one-on-one during class. We can actually talk with students about what they were thinking, what they meant, and how their writing could be stronger.

Through a writing workshop, writing becomes more like a practice and less like an often-stressful homework assignment disconnected from "real life." Once students experience the satisfaction of creating meaningful writing and are coached to form a habit of writing, they become relaxed with the writing process; they learn to trust it. The part of the brain that controls writing is like a muscle: it must be used to stay strong and limber. And, like muscles, once trained, it aches for movement! It needs regular practice. What happens when a person tries to run five miles once every month or two? Pain, discomfort. The body seizes up. However, the person who jogs peacefully two miles a day grows to love the sound of her feet on gravel and the blur of a dewy morning. This is what a workshop offers: the chance for students to grow comfortable with writing and viewing themselves as writers; the opportunity to enjoy picking up the familiar friends of pen and paper. Instead of experiencing the sick feeling of a surprise, high-stakes writing assignment, they take writing in stride, knowing the path they're on leads to meaningful, polished self-expression. They do not fear the process: their shoes are worn and broken in.

WRITING CLASS	WRITING WORKSHOP
All students work on the same prompt.	Students choose their own topics.
The focus is on the finished product.	The focus is on the entire writing process.
Most work is done outside of class.	All writing is done in class.
Students may not internalize corrections.	Teacher and student discuss written work together.
Production is the goal.	Practice is the goal.

Most educators agree that cultivating confident writers takes time and individualized student attention. And yet, it always seems so difficult to squeeze in time for writing, workshop-style, in our classes. Many of us have so many other tasks to complete under the umbrella of "English teachers." However, the need for solid writers, and hence for solid writing instruction, is not going away any time soon. Even if one ignores the personal benefits that come from learning how to express oneself meaningfully and clearly, we cannot deny the reality of writing assessments throughout a child's educational career.

What a Writing Workshop Looks Like

Before I address the question of "Where do I start?" I want to paint a picture of the goal: a running writing workshop. What does it look like when a class is actually participating in a writing workshop? There are many variations, but it generally follows the description on the next page.

Writing Workshop in Middle School © 2013 by Marilyn Pryle • Scholastic

A Writing Workshop in Motion

- When the bell rings, students are in their seats with their writing notebooks, and you start the day's mini-lesson. Students take notes and ask questions.

- After the mini-lesson, students begin a new writing assignment, or they resume work on a previous assignment: each student knows where he or she is in his or her work.

- Students check off completed tasks on their Assignment Sheets as they work. Each assignment consists of reading exemplary samples, answering questions about the samples, prewriting, writing a rough draft, revising, typing a final copy, and editing.

- Students work at both their desks and computers, depending on where they are in the assignment.

- You circulate around the room, checking in with some students and conferencing a bit longer with others.

- When an assignment is finished, students gather all their papers, put them in the proper order, clip them together, and place them in the "Papers to Be Graded" tray.

- If you have graded papers that students need to revise again, you return them as you circulate, and conference with them about what needs to be done.

- If you return a finished paper, the student records and files the piece in his or her Finished File.

- Later, during class, you might sit at your desk, reading papers and making yourself available for questions.

- All students continue thinking about, reading, writing, revising, typing, researching, editing, or filing their work.

- Students are free to approach you for help; they can look for information in any book or poster, or help themselves to paper or any other needed materials.

- You give students a one-minute warning before the end of class, so they can log off the computers, file any papers, and return their notebooks and other materials to the proper places. Everything is now ready for the following class.

A writing workshop in motion is a beautiful sight! And it is very attainable: When students are familiar with a routine and confident they can succeed, they will rise to meet our expectations. In addition, they will actually start to enjoy writing, and they will be proud of their creations.

Still, many teachers feel unsure. Even though we want to switch gears from a teacher-centered approach to writing to this student-centered, process-oriented approach, we don't know how to achieve this goal. Most of us must cover a huge amount of literature in our curriculums; even if we teach only writing, we must contend with large class sizes (an ideal workshop would have no more than fifteen) and numerical grades. Often we feel overwhelmed. I am constantly asked the question, "I want to run a writing workshop, but where do I start?"

Authenticity and Choice

Over the years, I have had the opportunity to teach English literature, writing, and English language learners in a variety of classroom settings. One of the most exciting of these assignments began when I got a job offer as an eighth-grade writing workshop teacher in a school district outside of Boston. I was told I would have five classes a day of up to 24 students per class, I would have to give numerical grades, and I would have to ready students for the persuasive essay on the state standardized tests. Other than that, I could teach writing in any way I thought best.

While considering these parameters, I knew what I did not want to do: I did not want to assign short prompts that left little room for exploration and growth. I did not want students to feel that the writing they did in my class was practice for "real" writing, pointless drills that counted for nothing but a grade. I did not want them to see the writers of published books as people living in a separate world, operating under a separate set of rules. I did not want students to merely write what they thought I wanted to read. I did not want them to simply "produce"—to robotically crank out essays, fiction, and poetry they did not care about and would immediately forget once grades were imposed.

I wanted students to write in genres they encountered in books, magazines, newspapers, and reliable Internet sources. I wanted them to write pieces that could be found in a mailbox or library. I wanted them to see their work within the framework of the massive amount of writing that people generate every day. And once they came to recognize that their writing was as real as any other writing that occurs in the world, I wanted them to learn to classify genres, genres within genres, and shades of genres. I wanted them to be experts at identification. And I wanted them to be, if not virtuosos, at least familiar with certain techniques employed within each genre.

Authenticity

For me, authenticity is twofold. First, it means that students write in real-world genres—pieces that one would actually encounter outside of school. When we look in a newspaper or magazine, or online, we see news stories, first-person narrations, opinion essays, and letters. When we read simply for our own enjoyment, we might turn to fiction. At the most poignant moments in our lives, many people seek the wisdom of poetry. As consumers, we may write letters of inquiry or complaint. As goal-oriented beings, we are often required to write persuasively about ourselves or our work. Many people must create analyses, reports, and studies for their

Authenticity

Students write the kind of pieces that could actually appear in a book, magazine, newspaper, or be placed in a mailbox, not "homework blurbs" derived from contrived, dead-end prompts.

Writing Workshop in Middle School © 2013 by Marilyn Pryle • Scholastic

jobs. These are just some of the genres of our lives. None of these are busywork; they are the modes we use to communicate and express ourselves. Authenticity, then, is having students craft pieces of writing that matter, that fit into our world.

Secondly, authenticity means that students feel a sense of ownership of their writing. It means they are not robotically answering prompts; the writing comes from somewhere within themselves. It reflects their beliefs, style, or learning. It has voice. Cultivating one's voice, of course, takes time and practice—and this is what a workshop setting provides.

A Note About Genre

When English teachers think of genre, we usually think of the main categories: fiction, nonfiction, poetry, and drama. However, as we know, these main genres can be broken down into subgenres: for example, nonfiction can include autobiography, news accounts, interviews, and research; poetry can be divided into formal poetry, free verse, concrete poetry, prose poetry, and so on. Subgenres vary not only in form but also in purpose. In teaching students to be writers, I want them to understand this. Therefore, in this book, when I use the word *genre*, I am referring not only to the major genres but also to any possible variation within them. And each assignment I give students is, in my mind, a slightly different genre (unless I purposefully repeat the same assignment at some point). For example, a set of first-quarter writing assignments (genres) might look like this:

1. Introductory Letter

2. Setting Sketch (autobiographical)

3. Free Verse Poem

4. Process (How-To) Essay

5. Character Sketch (autobiographical)

6. Reflection on a Reading

As you can see, most of these assignments could be put under the umbrella of nonfiction. However, they vary in form and purpose, and I want students to see the differences. When they get to high school, it will be important to understand how reflecting on reading is different from summarizing; likewise, an introductory letter will sound very different than a complaint letter to a corporation or a persuasive letter to a government official, though all are letters. A process essay will vary in purpose and organization from a compare-and-contrast essay or a persuasive essay, even though they are all, technically, essays. As writers, thinkers, and standardized test-takers, students must comprehend this. Thus, for me, the term *genre* refers to an infinite number of writing forms, each with its own slightly different purpose, format, or meaning.

> ### Genre
> Genre can refer to an infinite number of writing forms, each with its own slightly different purpose, format, or meaning.

Having students understand the *idea* of genre is critical, but so is organizing a writing workshop by specifically *ordering* the genres. Since students are more familiar with some genres than others, they find that writing in certain genres seems easier. Some genres do, in fact, require more sophisticated, subtle, or developed writing skills. Over time, I realized that I could arrange genres in a way that stacked skills as each genre progressed to the next. (I could demonstrate these skills directly via mini-lessons at the beginning of class.) For example, look again at my sample first-quarter list below. Next to each genre, I give an example of a skill that could be taught in a mini-lesson.

GENRE ASSIGNMENT*	SKILL
Introductory Letter	Brainstorming and Paragraphing
Setting Sketch (autobiographical)	Thinking of Sensory Details
Free Verse Poem	Form of a Poem
Process (How-To) Essay	Sequencing Paragraphs
Character Sketch (autobiographical)	Theme: Why This Person Matters
Reflection on a Reading	Giving an Opinion

* Throughout this book, I use the terms "genre," "genre assignments," and "assignments" interchangeably.

As this simple list shows, you can stack skills from assignment to assignment. For example, when students learn to brainstorm and group their information into paragraphs for an Introductory Letter, they can use that skill again for the Setting Sketch, Process Essay, Character Sketch, and Reflection on a Reading assignments. And when they write the process essay, they will not only form paragraphs, but also sequence them. Similarly, after they learn how to generate sensory details for a setting sketch, they will use that skill again for the free verse poem, process essay, and character sketch. I have found that if I purposefully order the genres and present one or two writing skills with each assignment, then reinforce each skill in future assignments, students get as much practice as possible in a scaffolded way.

> Genres can be placed in an order designed to stack skills and build learning.

This deliberate ordering of the genres ensures that students finish the year with some formal instruction in several genres and techniques, and gives the year a clear arc of progression. Techniques, strategies, and organizational patterns build upon one another; once a concept is taught, that knowledge is necessary for understanding the next genre or technique. Students will spiral through previously learned skills, combining them with new

> **Student Note**
>
> "I like trying different types of writing in school. The variety keeps assignments interesting."
>
> —Nick R.

Writing Workshop in Middle School © 2013 by Marilyn Pryle • Scholastic

techniques as they work through each assignment. Throughout this book, I will suggest genre assignments and skills that can be taught with them.

I want students to work mostly in class and at their own speed; however, I will have to plan for the very fast and the very slow writers. We do seven to eight pieces of writing, one for every three-day cycle. On each day of the cycle, I include one mini-lesson for a new assignment. Students who finish early can do "free-choice" assignments for extra credit, or writing assignments from other classes. Those who do not finish in class can work at home, during lunch, or after school. Otherwise, I assign no homework. Since most of the students do not want to take work home, this policy motivates them to keep writing throughout the class time.

I run my class like a true workshop: although I organize the workshop timeline, and regularly deliver bursts of whole-class instruction, students work independently and meet with me individually so I can personally advise, suggest, praise, and push. This one-on-one consultation is the heart of the workshop.

Choice

I'm the one who selects the genres, but I want students to feel like collaborators, like they have a choice in what they write. Thus, I have them choose their own topics for every assignment. It is both their decision and their responsibility. They cannot later complain that they did not want to write about baseball or the Grand Canyon or their first piano recital: they chose it, and if they didn't like it once they began to write, they could have chosen another topic. I want students to choose topics that are important to them; I want them to care about what they write. Feeling a connection to one's own writing is possibly the most important prerequisite of good writing. It motivates students to write clearly, organize, revise, and correct. It motivates them to sit in their chairs and find the right words, their words. It creates voice. If students do not care, on some level, in some way, about what they are writing, if students are simply going through the motions, everyone's time is wasted. For students to internalize any instruction at all, they have to *want* to successfully communicate what they are writing. And, just as important, I want students to see that they are experts in several areas, not only in their hobbies or talents, but also in their lives and passions. Only they can write what they have to write. This process of finding one's voice, of choosing one's own topics, of defining oneself through writing, is especially important for the adolescent in his or her search for identity.

My first task is to convince students that they actually have topics to write about; one way I do this is by beginning the year with a Topics for Writing

> ### Choice
> Students choose their own topics for every assignment. This establishes an emotional connection and a sense of responsibility.

> ### Student Note
> "The teacher should have a healthy mix of guidelines and freedom."
> —Brad S.

Student Note

"I like to choose my own topic because I can choose something I'm passionate about. This definitely leads to my best work."

—*Dan S.*

list, described fully in Chapter 6. I have to make students believe that any topic, written about in a genuine, thoughtful way, will be worthwhile to read, and that their individual perspectives can be interesting on the page.

Second, I have to earn students' trust as a reader and an advisor. If I am going to ask students to put their lives on the page—their beliefs, their memories, their reflections—if I am going to ask them to write with effort and honesty, then I have to be supportive, encouraging, and enthusiastic in my feedback and advice. I have to care about what they write every time I look at their writing. Sometimes this means that I have to invest energy reading about topics that could be clichés, shallow, or narcissistic—normal characteristics of early adolescent writing. I have to search earnestly for the nugget of truth within the writing and help the student build upon it.

My main goals, then, from the beginning, are to preserve the ideals of authenticity and choice, and balance them with practicality and necessity. I manage the number of students, the grades, the class time, and the preparation for the imminent state tests, but I also carve out a space for individuality and creativity, the silence at the center of the whirlwind where there is room for each student to think and grow. The following chapters will explain how I do it.

Student Note

"I like to be assigned a general topic and get to choose a sub-topic to write about. This way is my favorite because I still get to have freedom in my writing, but I don't have to choose from the whole wide world."

—*John C.*

Writing Workshop in Middle School © 2013 by Marilyn Pryle • Scholastic

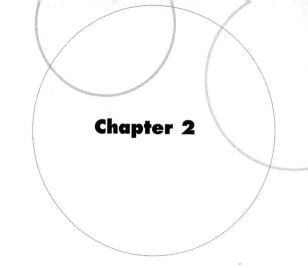

Chapter 2

Make a Plan: Genre Assignments

Of course, I realize that I don't need to advise teachers to plan. But unlike other subjects that come with textbooks and curriculums, writing is more internal, more personal, even if we are told to have students produce a certain type of essay or master a certain standard. Writing cannot simply be memorized; it cannot be crammed; and after a certain point, it cannot even be taught. It must be practiced. We can give tools and tips, we can give guidance as the process unfolds, but it is a personal art for each practitioner. If you feel drawn to a workshop approach for teaching writing, then you believe this, too. Writing is an individual journey. Therefore, we must plan in a slightly different way than we would for other disciplines. We must plan not only for the areas we want to cover, and for the various standards required; we must also plan for the writing journey.

A Note on Standards

Any list of state standards that I've ever seen, including the Common Core State Standards (CCSS), simply consists of the tenets of good writing broken down into specifics. These lists may vary slightly—genres highlighted by grade level, for example—but the main idea remains the same: that students learn to write clearly, purposefully, and with detail. By helping students develop various writing skills, find their voices, and become comfortable writing in several genres—all of which writing workshop provides—we will also be fulfilling the Common Core State Standards. Of course, to remain informed and focused, we should be familiar with the language of the CCSS, but I have found that a workshop approach naturally incorporates these standards and reinforces many reading-based standards as well.

Journeys take time. This is perhaps the biggest obstacle facing writing workshops: the time does not seem available, and the results often do not come quickly enough. But the knowledge gained from a workshop is something students learn on a deeper level, and is more permanent. It sharpens perception, clarifies thinking, and changes the way a person perceives the world. What is learned is not simply squeezed into students' short-term memory and spat back on a test; it is internalized and rooted; it continues to grow long after the workshop is over.

> Writing is not just a record of thought; it is an *extension* of thought. Often we do not know our true feelings about a topic until we begin writing about it.

Determine How Much Time You Have

The first question to ask yourself is, "How much time do I have to devote to this?" The answer is: it all depends on your situation. Maybe your time has already been set for you by administrators or the curriculum. Maybe you are trying to carve out a space in the curriculum yourself. Perhaps you have one class per week, or you can take part of a class for 20 or 30 minutes two or three times a week. Whatever the case, you'll need to quantify the number of classes or blocks of time you have available in a quarter, month, or week.

> **Brainstorm It!**
>
> How much time do you have to conduct a writing workshop in class?

Determine How Many Genre Assignments Most Students Can Do in a Given Time

In order to complete an assignment, students must progress through the writing process, either in class or at home. This includes understanding the genre-assignment, reading samples, prewriting, drafting, revising, editing, and, if necessary, revising again.

Based on this, try to establish how many assignments students can reasonably be expected to complete in a quarter. Determine how much in-time class you have and how much writing you will expect students to do outside of class.

> **Components of an Assignment**
> - Understanding of the genre-assignment
> - Reading samples
> - Prewriting
> - Drafting
> - Revising
> - Editing

Writing Workshop in Middle School © 2013 by Marilyn Pryle • Scholastic

If you have very little time, focus on making time in class to do the following:

- **Step 1:** Introduce the assignment.

- **Step 2:** Give a mini-lesson on one important aspect of the genre.

- **Step 3:** Have students prewrite or begin prewriting.

- **Step 4:** Meet with students individually after they have written a draft.

The first three steps can be done in one class period, or possibly even less, and the fourth will take a whole class once the assignment is under way. If you have a larger block of time (80 minutes, for example), you could spend a half hour or so setting up the new assignment and starting students on their prewriting, and the next 50 minutes circulating around the room, advising them on how to revise old papers, and answering questions about the new assignment. Most of the actual writing and subsequent revising would be done at home.

Decide what your students can realistically be expected to complete in the course of one quarter, but at the same time, don't worry! You can always change your plan as you go along, adding or subtracting assignments based upon the pace of students.

Not a lot of time? Try this:

1 class:

- Introduce assignment.

- Focus mini-lesson on one key aspect of genre.

- Students prewrite.

Homework (2–3 days):

- Students write a draft, revise it, and bring in a typed copy.

Read and comment on drafts (2–3 days).

1 class:

- Begin new assignment.

- Return previous drafts; students revise them while working on new assignment.

- Meet with students individually.

TOTAL: 1 class per week

Brainstorm It!

Look at your calendar and estimate how many assignments your students can do in a quarter. You can always add or subtract assignments as the quarter progresses.

	EXAMPLE	YOUR ESTIMATE
How much time do you have each week?	two 45-minute blocks	
When/where will students write?	class / home	
How many assignments can students do?	1 every 3 classes	
Total number of assignments per quarter:	5 (w / extra time)	

Remember, recommending a certain number of assignments for all students does not diminish the individuality of the work. Each student will write, revise, and grow differently and at his or her own pace. Requiring students to complete a certain number, or certain kinds, of assignments creates uniformity, fairness, and scaffolded progress. Using rubrics (see Chapter 7) allows us to give grades that reflect both the personal and the public, the development of the art and the acquisition of the tools.

Choose the Genre Assignments Students Will Complete

The next step is to decide which genres will best serve your overall goal. Ask yourself what you want students to be able to do by the end of the year. Should you emphasize essay writing? Should you use the time to help students understand narrative and poetry from the inside out? Should you do a little of everything? Let your larger goals guide your choice of genres.

Writing Workshop in Middle School © 2013 by Marilyn Pryle • Scholastic

Possible Goals for Writing Workshop

Exposure to several genres

Persuasive writing fluency

Writing about literature

Standardized test preparation

Autobiographical expression

Exposure to research-based writing

Writing fiction

Writing poetry

Essay writing

Brainstorm It!

What is your goal (or goals) for writing workshop in your class(es)? What do you want your students to know by the end of the year?

When you have the end in mind, it is easier to find a path to get there. Roughly choose which genre assignments will take students to the desired destination, whether it be a solid persuasive essay or overall exposure to many kinds of writing. I say "roughly" because, of course, the plan may need to change as the year progresses.

Build the Complexity of the Genre-Assignments

The most important consideration when choosing and ordering assignments is that you try to have each assignment increase in complexity and difficulty. That is, each assignment should build on the ones before it. This way, students will have to constantly utilize what they have learned while they add to that base. For example, organizing the ideas from a haphazard brainstorm into groups might take some effort in the beginning of the year, but after doing it ten or twenty or thirty times, it becomes routine for students. Finding the small details in a setting or an idea may seem arduous at first, but when the mind is trained to search for details, they will easily materialize. My goal with writing workshop is to make students self-sufficient writers; I know they will not have me coaching them throughout their writing lives. A one-time lesson on transition words or strong verbs or cohesive paragraphs will not train the mind. Only practice and repetition will create lasting habits.

> Arrange your assignments so that each assignment increases in difficulty and builds on the previous ones. This way, students practice learned skills while trying new techniques with each lesson.

A chart of several possible genre assignments appears on the next page. They are categorized based on the most common goals; you will notice that some assignments are repeated since they fall into more than one category. I have also categorized the assignments by level of difficulty, and even within these categories are further divisions based on difficulty. With guidance, students should be able to complete the easy assignments at the beginning of the year and work their way to the advanced assignments with practice. Genre assignments that don't obviously fit into the categories but that deserve mention are listed in the "Other" category. I should stress that this is a chart of *possible* assignments and skills—you can reach your goal without doing all of them!

Writing Workshop in Middle School © 2013 by Marilyn Pryle • Scholastic

POSSIBLE GENRE ASSIGNMENTS

DIFFICULTY	ESSAY-WRITING	NARRATION	LITERATURE-BASED	POETRY	OTHER
EASY	Introductory Letter Descriptive Essay Autobiographical Essay Process Essay Classification Essay	Setting Sketch Character Sketch Autobiographical Essay Newspaper Account	Setting Sketch Character Sketch Autobiographical Essay Eyewitness Account Free Verse Poem	Free Verse Poem Ode	Thank-You Letter Memo Free Choice (Any)
INTERMEDIATE	Compare/Contrast Essay Persuasive Essay Letter for Social Change Analysis of a Short Story Test Writing With Prompt	Retelling of Legend Ballad Children's Book Analysis of a Short Story Short Story	Retelling of Legend Ballad Reflection Paper Analysis of a Short Story Short Story	Ballad Children's Book	Business Letter Résumé Letter of Submission for Publication Travel Brochure
ADVANCED	Book Review Personal Essay Arts Review Research Paper Analysis of a Poem	Historical Fiction Science Fiction Longer Fiction/Novel Beginning Drama	Historical Fiction Science Fiction Analysis of a Poem Rhyming Poem Poems in Various Forms (sonnet, sestina, villanelle) Parody Drama	Analysis of Poem Rhyming Poem Poems in Various Forms (sonnet, sestina, villanelle) Parody	Article From Interview Cover Letter for Résumé/Application

Remember that not all genre assignments need to be completed in order to reach your goals. Many of these assignments involve overlapping skills. Take a minute to examine the short descriptions of each genre assignment on pages 145–151, as well as the corresponding skills. Notice how many of the skills are repeated in various assignments. So, even if you only have time for a few assignments a quarter, you can strategically choose ones that will focus on the skills that you consider important for your students.

In addition, you can see how these overlapping skills can be layered upon one another as students progress from the easy genre assignments to the intermediate and advanced. For example, let's say one of your goals is to have students understand the workings of fiction and write a well-developed short story by the end of the first semester. You know that you can find time for four assignments a quarter. One path to achieve that is shown below.

GENRE ASSIGNMENT	SKILLS
1. Setting Sketch (autobiographical)	Generating sensory details; paragraphing
2. Character Sketch (autobiographical)	Sensory details; dialogue; rudimentary theme
3. Autobiographical Account	All the above, plus plot; more developed theme
4. Retelling of a Legend	All the above, plus narrative voice
5. Contemporary Short Story	All the above, plus character motivation
6. Historical Fiction	All the above in a historical context (research required)
7. Science Fiction	All the above within sci-fi parameters
8. Free-Choice Fiction	Reiteration of all skills

You can see how a Setting Sketch (which draws primarily from sensory detail) would be easier to write than a Character Sketch (which involves not only sensory detail but also dialogue and actions), and how both sketches would prefigure an Autobiographical Account (which incorporates setting and character descriptions as well as plot and theme). Thinking further, one can see how autobiography could foreshadow fiction, and that a short story set in the present day could prepare students for historical or science fiction.

I'm not saying that it is necessarily easier for a person to write autobiography than historical fiction. Certainly, writing a sophisticated, well-wrought memoir is an art. However, as teachers, we can present these genres in a way that lends itself to practicing basic skills first before moving to more complex tasks. It is easier to introduce the idea of

Writing Workshop in Middle School © 2013 by Marilyn Pryle • Scholastic

sensory detail in a basic setting sketch of a familiar place than it is in a piece of science fiction, which would also require developing characters operating in an interesting plot that reveals a meaningful theme, all within a well-researched scientific framework.

Let's try this again with a different goal in mind. Let's say you can only do eight or twelve assignments over the whole year (two or three a quarter), and your goal is solely to prepare students for an upcoming standardized test essay. You could choose this path from the Essay-Writing column of the chart on page 21.

GENRE ASSIGNMENT	SKILLS
1. Introductory Letter	Brainstorming and grouping ideas
2. Process Essay	Sequential organization with transition words
3. Compare/Contrast Essay	Compare/contrast organization; concluding with persuasion
4. Persuasive Essay	Fact vs. opinion; thesis
5. Letter for Social Change	Writing a strong introduction and conclusion
6. Analysis of a Short Story	Developing a thesis about literature
7. Book Review	Developing a personal opinion about literature
8. Personal Essay	Supporting a thesis with various sources
9. Arts Review	Developing a personal opinion about the arts
10. Test Writing With Prompt	Understanding prompts

You can see how beginning with an Introductory Letter assignment and grounding the students in brainstorming and paragraphing would benefit them throughout the subsequent assignments. Likewise, it would make sense to have students write a process essay, which is organized sequentially, before a compare-and-contrast essay, which requires more adept organization and thinking. Similarly, analyzing the literary elements of a short story might seem more manageable to students than developing a review of an entire novel for the book review. Notice too that genre assignments 4–10 are all persuasive in nature. Thus, after learning the basics of purpose, audience, and structure, students would spend several assignments exploring forms of persuasion, practicing their persuasive skills, and hopefully becoming more prepared for the test.

Let's try another goal: if you wanted to expose students to writing narrative and poetry but you only had time for a dozen or so assignments and had standardized tests in the spring, I would recommend the following approach.

THE STANDARDIZED SAMPLER

GENRE ASSIGNMENT	SKILLS
1. Introductory Letter or Descriptive Essay	Brainstorming and grouping ideas; sensory details
2. Setting Sketch	Sensory details; paragraphing; theme
3. Free Verse Poem or Ode	Sensory details; similes; onomatopoeia; theme
4. Character Sketch	Sensory details; dialogue; theme
5. Process Essay	Sequential organization with transition words
6. Compare/Contrast Essay	Compare/contrast organization, using persuasion in conclusion
7. Autobiographical Account	Details; plot; dialogue; more developed theme
8. Ballad (family or historical)	Details; plot in poetry; poetic form
9. Persuasive Essay	Differentiation of fact vs. opinion; thesis
10. Letter for Social Change	Writing a strong introduction and conclusion
11. Arts Review or Book Review	Developing an opinion about literature/arts
12. Personal Essay	Supporting a thesis with reasoning; autobiography; literature; research

I call this the standardized sampler because the first eight assignments give a sampling of narrative, poetry, and basic essay writing while building up skills such as using description and organizing. This readies students for the final four essays of the course, all of which are formally persuasive (the commonly targeted genre of standardized tests).

In the next chapter on mini-lessons, I will return to this list and fully explain the group

Writing Workshop in Middle School © 2013 by Marilyn Pryle • Scholastic

of skills that can be taught through it. However, by just looking at the list itself, one can see how the setting sketch and character sketch prefigure the autobiographical account, and how all three prepare the student for the ballad, as does the free verse poem. Likewise, once students have written a persuasive essay, they will be well equipped to write a letter for social change and an art or book review. Finally, the personal essay would draw upon elements of persuasion, narrative, and a bit of research, thereby tying several genres together nicely.

An easy version of the workshop, one that could be used by elementary teachers or ELL teachers, would start with autobiographical narrative and progress to an introduction of persuasive writing. Here is one version of that path.

A BEGINNER'S WORKSHOP

GENRE ASSIGNMENT	SKILLS
1. Setting Sketch	Generating sensory details
2. Character Sketch	Sensory details; introduction to theme
3. Ode	Sensory details; similes; onomatopoeia; theme
4. Autobiographical Incident	Details; plot: more developed theme
5. Retelling of a Legend (family or cultural)	Same as #4, plus third-person narration
6. Children's Book	All the above, plus elements of a story
7. Friendly Letter	Brainstorming and paragraphing
8. Compare-and-Contrast Essay	Organizing a compare/contrast essay; using persuasion to conclude
9. Travel Brochure	Basic persuasion with reasons
10. Letter to Principal (a version of the Letter for Social Change)	Thesis supported by reason paragraphs

These lists are just some ideas about how to string assignments together; the possibilities are limitless (see Chapter 10 for a discussion of assignments and skills to complement a literature class). Again, the main idea is to teach each assignment based on the assignment(s) that came before it.

Spend some time looking at the suggestions on these lists, keeping your goals in mind. Also, notice which assignments seem exciting, fun, or interesting to you. Then reread the goals you brainstormed and your estimated amount of time for writing. You can start small—maybe with just one quarter or just assignments that look manageable and fit your overall vision.

I should note some thoughts here. First, do not feel that the assignments on these charts are the only possible assignments or that the skills presented with each one are the only ones that can be taught with a particular assignment. You can add, rearrange, or modify any genre assignment on these charts to your own liking and based on your expertise. I offer these charts as a starting point; the stepping stones within them are based on my own experience.

> It can be beneficial to repeat certain genre assignments in the course of the year.

Second, feel free to repeat genre assignments: for example, I've had students repeat the easy character sketch as part of their brainstorming for the advanced genre of historical fiction. Likewise, it can be interesting and fruitful, for example, for students to write in one of the easy genres, like a free verse poem, after completing an advanced form like a sonnet or villanelle. Such repetition heightens their sense of the form of free verse and fosters writing at a deeper level. This is true of all the genre assignments suggested in this book; revisiting any genre with the intent of deeper exploration is always beneficial. However, if the goal is to expose your students to a wide range of genres, time unfortunately doesn't permit much repetition. For that reason, I like to keep a standing offer of a free-choice assignment at the

> Your enthusiasm for the genres themselves, and the order in which you present them, is one of the most important elements of the class.

end of each quarter or semester. Students can return anew to any genre to which they feel particularly drawn. Likewise, they could write a letter of submission (in which they offer a piece of writing for publication) at the end of each semester.

As you look over these genres, you might be thinking that you personally would teach some of them in a different order. Go for it! Do what seems logical to you. It all depends on which facets of each assignment you wish to focus on. For example, you can have students write a very simple version of an analysis of a poem or arts review. As long as the techniques and skills you present grow in difficulty, and you hold students accountable for learning them in all future assignments (via a rubric, discussed in Chapter 7), feel free to order your assignments in a way that inspires you. Your passion for the genres and their order (your overall vision for the workshop) is one of the most important elements of the class.

How to Start Small

If choosing ten or more assignments for the year seems daunting, choose your first two assignments. Pick assignments that seem manageable and that fit into your overall vision, skill-wise. When you've selected two, then choose two more. Build as you go.

* * *

Like all learning, learning writing grows best in small increments that are allowed to take root and grow over time. This growth comes with the constant reinforcement that naturally happens when assignments are deliberately chosen and carefully ordered. But even more important, students will gain confidence from this incremental approach. Throughout the year, there will be a steady stream of prior knowledge coming from past assignments. Students will feel like they have a head start on new assignments because they are simply practicing all they already know, just in a different format. By the spring, they will be experts in the skills they learned early in the year, such as generating sensory detail and grouping similar ideas together. My goal with the writing workshop is that these skills become so ingrained that students won't ever shake them; that years from now, even if they are not writing, they will not be able to ignore, for example, the sights, sounds, and smells around them; that they will not be able to stop similar ideas from naturally clustering in their minds.

Chapter 3

Make a Plan: Mapping the Mini-Lessons

At this point, you should have a general idea of how certain skills can be pinpointed within each genre assignment. Now it's time to map these main skills in the form of mini-lessons, along with any additional mini-lessons in content, craft, mechanics, and spelling. Remember, the workshop should always be viewed as a work in progress, and you may decide to change your mini-lesson, genre assignment, or even your overall vision depending on how your students progress through the assignments. I should also note that I use the term "mini-lesson" loosely—some of my mini-lessons take much longer than a few minutes, especially when students are beginning a new genre assignment. My goal is to limit mini-lessons to five to ten minutes, and most do fall into that time frame; however, some topics do creep into the fifteen minute range. Some topics simply take longer to explain, and students will still have time to write. If I know I have a long mini-lesson scheduled for one day, I will try to balance it with a shorter mini-lesson the next day. With that said, I usually teach three mini-lessons per assignment. They mostly follow this pattern:

- **Mini-lesson #1**: Introduction to the genre assignment/discussion of organization and applicable prewriting techniques
- **Mini-lesson #2**: A skill related to the content of the genre assignment
- **Mini-lesson #3**: A skill related to writing craft and mechanics, including spelling

> **Mini-Lesson:**
> Five to ten minutes of direct instruction on one specific skill or topic. Students can immediately incorporate this new knowledge into their writing.

 Writing Workshop in Middle School © 2013 by Marilyn Pryle • Scholastic

Mini-Lesson #1

My first mini-lesson for an assignment is usually an introduction to the genre itself. I talk with students about how the genre differs from other genres, how it is organized, or, in some cases such as a poem, letter, children's book, or brochure, its physical aspects. I always give students one or two good examples of the genre to peruse, so they understand the end goal. The rest of this class is usually devoted to choosing topics and doing some form of prewriting.

Mini-Lesson #2

The second mini-lesson tends to focus on some aspect of the content of the piece. You might discuss how to use figurative language or develop a theme, or you can present ways to write an effective introduction or a strong clincher.

Mini-Lesson #3

The third mini-lesson is usually an exploration of a specific writing habit or convention. With the setting sketch, for example, I often teach a short mini-lesson on what I call "banned words," which is discussed on the next page.

Of course, this is only a broad plan, and many variations exist. For example, if the genre is very new or complex, I might not do a mini-lesson on craft or grammar and instead do all three mini-lessons on characteristics of the genre.

What if you can't do three mini-lessons?

Remember that many combinations of mini-lessons are possible! Do not feel like you must have three or that they must be spaced out day by day. Depending on your available time, you can double up mini-lessons or only teach two (or even one) for each assignment. Likewise, with *more* time, you can teach more than three mini-lessons.

What's in a Mini-Lesson?

I try to keep mini-lessons mini. I communicate the key information using simple, direct language, and I use a few examples to illustrate. That's all. When students enter the class, they grab their notebooks, and I write the mini-lesson topic on the board. (For a discussion of notebooks, see page 37.) They record the topic in the notebook's table of contents, take notes on the topic and examples, and then they get to writing. The mini-lessons also incorporate interaction with students (for example, by tapping prior knowledge). A sample mini-lesson on banned words appears on the next page.

Mini-Lesson: Banned Words

I write the following words on the board:

good	*awesome*	*thing(s)*
bad	*cool*	*item(s)*
great	*nice*	*kind of*
sort of	*boring*	*stuff*

Ms. P.: OK, everyone. Look at these words on the board. What do you think about them?

Jamie: They're good words?

Mark: They're words we use a lot?

Ms. P.: They're definitely words we use a lot, right? But do they help us in writing?

Kelly: Well, yeah, if we use them a lot, we need them for writing. If something's good or bad, you have to say it.

Ms. P.: Let me ask you this: If you saw a movie, and the next day your friend asked you how it was, and you said "good," what does that mean?

Jamie: That you liked it.

Ms. P.: Yes, but does it tell us anything about the movie itself?

Frank: That it was good. (*This discussion is proving my point about the words themselves!*)

Ms. P.: Anyone, what's your favorite kind of movie?

Mark: Action.

Kelly: Romance, with a happy ending!

Tyler: Scary movies.

Vicky: Comedy. I hate scary movies.

Frank: Murder mysteries!

Ms. P.: OK, so what's "good" to one person might not be "good" to another, right? Tyler might like a movie with a villain wearing a ski mask and carrying a machete going around town—

Vicky: No! I hate that stuff!

Ms. P.: And Kelly would like a movie about people falling in love, getting separated somehow, and finding their way back to each other—

Frank: Boooorrrriinnng.

Ms. P.: So do you see how these words really *don't* have precise meaning? We use them so much that their meanings are muddled. They're not specific enough. Now, in speaking, I know even I use these words a lot. But in writing, we should all try to avoid them. So, for this year, I'm declaring a ban on these words. The words on the board are officially banned in all your writing for this year.

Writing Workshop in Middle School © 2013 by Marilyn Pryle • Scholastic

Mark:	What?!
Jamie:	What are we supposed to say?
Ms. P.:	Well, that's just it. Say the *exact* words, not these easy, lazy words without any meaning! Let's try it: What if you said, "My locker has a lot of stuff in it." "Stuff" is now banned. What else could you say?
Jamie:	"Things." (*This happens* **every** *time I teach this lesson.*)
Ms. P.:	Banned.
Frank:	"Items."
Ms. P.:	Banned. Try this, everyone. On a piece of paper, write down whatever is actually in your locker right now. Make a list. Go. (*I give them a minute.*) What do you have?
Mark:	Books, my jacket, my lacrosse stick, my lunch, my ski hat, a note from Kelly taped to the side, a bunch of papers jammed at the bottom . . .
Ms. P.:	OK. Now that's much more interesting than saying, "I have some stuff in my locker," isn't it? How about some others? (*I call on one or two more kids.*) See, naming the things is more interesting and specific than saying "things." Saying the movie was "terrifying but funny in parts and, since the hero survived, hopeful" gives us more information than just saying, "It was good." This is your job as a writer: to be specific. To say the exact word. To name things. OK? So we'll try it this year. If you're ever totally stuck thinking of a new word, just ask me and I'll help you.

Banned Words! poster in the classroom

Frank:	Can we use the words when this year is over?
Ms. P.:	Well, I can't stop you from doing that. But by then you'll be so convinced that you won't want to!

Throughout the year, students correct me if I use any of these words in my speech. These are wonderful teaching moments, as students watch me search for a better word. For now, I don't bombard them with other examples of the banned words in action since ample opportunities will arise in their own writing as the year progresses, and it is more effective to work on each student's individual uses.

Student Note

"Changing banned words makes your paper look like a 10th grader wrote it instead of a 4th grader."

—Kevin S.

Mini-Lesson: Tone

Here's a mini-lesson on tone that I usually do a bit later in the year:

Ms. P.:   Who can explain what the word *tone* means?

Ashley: It's when you play an instrument—what it sounds like.

Ms. P.:   Good! It has something to do with the quality of a sound, right? Has anyone ever had your mom or dad say, "Don't take that tone with me!" (*Almost everyone raises his or her hand.*) What does that mean?

Jack: It means you're being sarcastic or angry.

Ms. P.:   Good—it means something about the feeling in your voice, doesn't it? (*scattered nods*) OK. What if you ask a friend how his or her day was, and your friend says, "Oh, it was just great!" (*I say this in a genuinely happy and eager voice.*) What do you think happened?

Cecile: Something good. Maybe a high test grade or good news.

Ms. P.:   Right. Now, what if you ask the same question on another day, and your friend says, "Oh, it was just great!" (*I say this sentence with a growl, rolling my eyes.*) What does this mean?

Jamie: That really it was bad.

Ms. P.:   Right! Now, how is that possible? Both times, the same five words were used: *Oh. It. Was. Just. Great.* So how can those words have two opposite meanings?

Nate: It depends on *how* you say it, like, sarcastically or happily.

Ms. P.:   Excellent. That's tone. Do you see how tone contributes to the meaning? Now, even though you can't hear the author's voice when you read, you can still sense his or her tone. Look at the first two sentences on the board. Imagine a writer is reviewing a band's newest release, and in the middle of the article he says this:

    The incessant bass and screechy vocals make this a punishment for your ears. If you like headaches and cacophony, then rush to the store to buy this CD.

Ms. P.:   What's the tone here?

Cecile: Sarcastic.

Ms. P.:   How do you know?

Cecile: He says to buy it, but only if you like headaches.

Ms. P.:   Excellent! What other words in these sentences are negative?

Steve: *Screechy.*

Chloe: *Punishment.*

Ms. P.:   Yes. Now, you might not know what *cacophony* means, but does it sound positive or negative?

Class:	Negative.
Ms. P.:	Right. It means "many discordant sounds mixed together." Now look at the next sentences:

The steady beat balances well with the singer's high, angelic voice. The blend is like heaven meeting Earth. If you enjoy music that differs from the boring mainstream sound, then this CD is for you.

Ms. P.:	What's the tone here? What's the author's feeling behind the words?
Chloe:	He likes the CD.
Ms. P.:	How do you know?
Chloe:	He uses "angelic" and "heaven," and says that other music is boring.
Ms. P.:	Excellent. Now think about this: Could both of these sentences be about the *same* CD? (*Students nod.*) The way we tell them apart is by their tone. So, what could we say is an accurate definition for tone in writing?
Jamie:	The writer's feeling.
Ashley:	The good or bad vocabulary the writer uses.
Ms. P.:	Great. Let's try this (*I write on board*):

Tone: the writer's attitude toward the subject, shown through word choice and images

Now I want you to think about tone when you write. Ask yourself: "Is my tone how I want it to sound? Is it too sarcastic or angry? Is it humorous when I want it to be serious, or vice versa? What can I change to make it sound more like what I want?"

It will take some time—years probably—for students to fully understand and master tone. But as with most of our topics during the year, I am satisfied even if students only become mindful that these concepts exist. We will revisit tone in our final preparation for the standardized tests so that any potential negative attitudes about the test itself don't make it into the students' writing (see page 129).

Plan Your Mini-Lessons

The chart on page 34 shows possible mini-lessons, grouped into categories and listed by difficulty. Of course, this is not a definitive list; nor should you feel like you must cover every single mini-lesson. Depending on class level, class time, and your class's individual needs, choose the mini-lessons you feel will best serve your students. Throughout this chapter are examples of how certain mini-lessons fit the genre assignments listed in the previous chapter. The appendix contains a full list of all genre assignments matched with possible mini-lessons—so don't be intimidated by the number of mini-lessons on the chart on the next page! Simply take a minute to read through them and try to sense how the easier mini-lessons in each column progress into the more advanced ones.

POSSIBLE MINI-LESSONS BY CATEGORY AND ORDER OF DIFFICULTY

DIFFICULTY	ORGANIZATION	CONTENT	CRAFT	MECHANICS/SPELLING
EASY	Brainstorming/Grouping Webbing Venn Diagram How to Set Up a Letter Brainstorming a Character Sequential Organization (Process) Free Verse/Line Breaks Chronological Organization Organizing an Interview Article	Using Sensory Details Introductions: Ways to Start Essays Conclusions: Ways to End Essays Similes Onomatopoeia Personification Alliteration Five W's of a Newspaper Article Elements of Characterization (Looks, Does, Says) Theme Introductions: Ways to Start Narrative Conclusions: Ways to End Narrative Creating Interview Questions	Banned Words Editing/Revising Checklist Freewriting Avoiding You Avoiding Clichés Words Instead of *Said* Transition Words Sentence Variation	Writing an Address Homophones Apostrophes Quoting Dialogue Maintaining Tense Addressing an Envelope
INTERMEDIATE	Two Ways of Organizing a Compare/Contrast Essay Organizing Persuasion Organizing a Personal Essay Organizing an Analysis	Fact vs. Opinion Persuasive Topics Persuasive Clinchers Topics for Social Change Parts of a Short Story Test-Taking Tips How to Reflect on Literature Choosing a Narrative Voice Character Motivation	Creating a Thesis Audience Awareness Researching a Legend Summarizing Titles Strong Verbs Tone Mood Using Rhyme Using Meter	Run-ons Fragments How to Use a Comma Subject-Verb Agreement Pronoun Agreement Quoting a Source How to Quote a Poem/Song
ADVANCED	Organizing a Research Paper Organizing a Business Letter Setting Up a Script	Elements of a Book Review Developing an Opinion About Literature Rhyme Scheme Mapping Meter Linking Form and Content in Poetry Stage Directions	How to Use a Quotation Dictionary Paraphrasing Conducting Research Researching History Researching Science Goals in Parody Publishing Your Writing	Colons Semicolons Citing a Source in-Text Works Cited

Writing Workshop in Middle School © 2013 by Marilyn Pryle • Scholastic

You can see how several mini-lessons relate to certain genre assignments; for example, a mini-lesson on theme would be particularly useful for writing the Autobiographical Essay assignment; a mini-lesson about onomatopoeia would be helpful during the Ode assignment. In addition, many of the mini-lessons in the Organization category would naturally be taught when the assignment is introduced; a mini-lesson on how to set up a letter, for example, might be necessary before students begin to write a friendly letter.

Like Assignments, Mini-Lessons Build in Complexity

The goal is to teach the mini-lessons so that they build on one another, with students first ingesting smaller, more basic ideas before moving on to larger, more complex concepts. For example, in the beginning of the year, I always fit a Sensory Details mini-lesson into one of my first assignments (usually in the Setting Sketch assignment, as I mentioned earlier). Employing sensory detail is a fundamental skill that can be used throughout the year and beyond, but it especially becomes useful when, much later, I teach a mini-lesson on mood. (One of the ways writers create mood is through the deliberate selection of sensory details in the setting.)

Simplicity Means Choosing

The three-mini-lesson method (or two, or four, whatever you choose) requires some control on your part. You cannot teach every minute detail of every assignment. You must focus on the most important aspects of an assignment and let the rest go! This can be difficult for teachers, whose job it is, after all, to teach well and seize upon all teachable moments. However, bombarding students with every single writerly bit of information during the very first assignment, and every assignment after that, will consume all writing time and deaden spirits. So we must choose and grade only a few select concepts at a time.

Just because I don't teach every relevant point about a genre, doesn't mean students aren't learning these concepts anyway. Additionally, during individual conferencing, you can add the aspects a student is ready to hear. For example, during the Setting Sketch assignment, I might teach mini-lessons on sensory details—a basic idea of the theme—and on banned words. Students may not have had a formal mini-lesson on paragraphing, but that wouldn't stop me from pointing out in individual conferences that a certain sentence doesn't seem to fit with the rest of the paragraph. Or, even though I may not teach a mini-lesson on introductions, if a student has written a wonderful setting sketch with a lackluster first sentence, I might ask which sensory detail would be most exciting to begin with and suggest it be moved up.

Of course, once an idea is taught it must be remembered, so the information piles up very quickly. The difference here is in the *way* it piles up. Instead of hurling every possible

> You must force yourself to focus only on the most important aspects of an assignment and let the rest go. Trust in the process.

concept at students for each assignment, the small-chunk/linked-learning method keeps concepts orderly and manageable.

Combining and Repeating Mini-Lessons

Depending on the class or topic, I might combine some of the mini-lessons listed above. When presenting a genre assignment such as the ode to a class that already has completed a Free Verse Poem assignment and thus has been exposed to the basics of poetry, I could have a longer mini-lesson on figurative language instead of separate mini-lessons on similes, personification, and onomatopoeia. Or, when introducing the Letter for Social Change assignment, I might take an extra 60 seconds to show the class what an addressed envelope should look like. At the same time, if I've chosen to combine mini-lessons, but as I'm teaching realize that I'm infringing on writing time, I will change plans and save a portion of the lesson to teach later.

I sometimes repeat mini-lessons, either to reinforce an important skill or technique, to add to it, or to view it from a new vantage. For example, when teaching the process essay early in the year, I do a mini-lesson on transition words of addition and chronology (*first, then, next, finally, also, additionally*). A bit later, when teaching the compare-and-contrast essay, I remind students of the transition words we have looked at and then present transition words of contrast (*however, although, on the other hand*). Likewise, during instruction for the Social Action Letter assignment, I focus on tone; later in the year, I like to revisit tone during Arts Review and Parody assignments to reinforce an understanding of its role and examine it from different angles.

> It can be helpful to repeat mini-lessons at certain points during the year, deepening the concept each time.

Conventions

You may have noticed that in the chart on page 34, I've included only a few mini-lessons on conventions (the ones students struggle with most often), but this does not mean that I ignore conventions. On the contrary, I start grammar instruction with the first assignment of the year, during individual conferences. Working one-on-one with students enables me to give the grammar lesson each of them needs with a particular piece of work as the clay. As the year progresses, I use mini-lessons when I see that most of my students are battling a particular issue related to basic mechanics.

Writing Notebooks

It is my dream that mini-lessons become ingrained in my students' minds and hearts for all future intellectual use and personal growth. In the meantime, I have students keep a special notebook in which they can record the important points of each mini-lesson. They create a table of contents and put each mini-lesson on a new page. (See Chapter 6 for a full explanation on setting up the notebooks with students.)

Tip

If possible, store notebooks in the classroom so students can grab them on the way in and replace them on the way out. This provides students with easy access to old mini-lessons whenever they need to refer to them. And by the end of the year, each student has a writing handbook to take into the next school year and beyond.

Table of Contents	
Topics for writing	1
Brainstorming and Grouping	5
Using Sensory Details	6
Transition Words	7
Theme	8
Banned Words	9
Free Verse	10
Simile/Onomatopoeia	11
Avoiding Clichés	13
Elements of Characterization	14
Quoting Dialogue	15
Ways to Begin an Essay	16
Maintaining Tense	18
Chronological Organization	19
Theme (Part 2)	20
Words Instead of "said"	21
Rhyme Scheme	23
Mapping metaphors	24
Titles	25
Fact Vs. Opinion	26
Organizing Persuasion	27
Avoiding "you"	28
Topics for social change	29

Possible Mini-Lessons: Standardized Sampler

On the next page is a list of twelve possible mini-lessons to accompany the Standardized Sampler assignments in the previous chapter.

If you did these twelve assignments—just three per quarter—your students would have practiced a lot of writing by the end of the year. Having exposure to different genres, developing a sense of voice, and becoming familiar with different prewriting and organizational techniques, they would be poised to write a research paper.

Remember, though, that this list is just a *possible* combination of assignments and mini-lessons. Although some mini-lessons are explicitly related to the genre assignment itself (such as Two Ways to Organize a Compare/Contrast Essay), many other mini-lessons could work with several genres. For example, it would be productive to teach how to write conclusions during the Compare-and-Contrast Essay assignment, since this essay offers several ending possibilities, but the topic could also be taught during another assignment if it seems to work better in your overall curriculum. Choosing assignments and then linking them together with mini-lessons is like fitting together a giant puzzle, with some pieces that are stationary and some that could fit in a couple of different places. How your puzzle takes shape depends entirely on your preferences and situation.

STANDARDIZED SAMPLER MINI-LESSONS

1. Introductory Letter or Descriptive Essay	**1.** How to Set up a Letter/Brainstorming & Grouping (whole class) **2.** Using Sensory Details **3.** Transition Words (addition)
2. Setting Sketch	**1.** Intro to Setting Sketch/Brainstorming **2.** Theme (basic) **3.** Banned Words
3. Free Verse Poem or Ode	**1.** Intro to Free Verse/Freewriting **2.** Simile and Onomatopoeia **3.** Avoiding Clichés
4. Character Sketch	**1.** Brainstorming a Character **2.** Elements of Characterization **3.** Quoting Dialogue
5. Process Essay	**1.** Intro to Process Essay/Sequential Organization **2.** Ways to Begin an Essay **3.** Maintaining Tense
6. Compare/ Contrast Essay	**1.** Two Ways to Organize a Compare-and-Contrast Essay **2.** Ways to End an Essay **3.** Transition Words (contrasting)
7. Autobiographical Account	**1.** Intro to Autobiography/Review of Brainstorming Character & Setting **2.** Theme (developed) **3.** Words Instead of *Said*
8. Ballad (Family or Historical)	**1.** What is a Ballad? **2.** Rhyme Scheme **3.** Titles
9. Persuasive Essay	**1.** Fact vs. Opinion/Organizing Persuasion **2.** Persuasive Topics **3.** Sentence Variation
10. Letter for Social Change	**1.** Introduction to Letter for Social Change/Topics for Social Change **2.** Persuasive Clinchers **3.** Audience
11. Arts Review or Book Review	**1.** How to Develop an Opinion About Literature/Arts **2.** Tone **3.** Avoiding "You"
12. Personal Essay	**1.** Personal Essay Defined/Organizing a Personal Essay **2.** Summarizing **3.** Quoting a Source

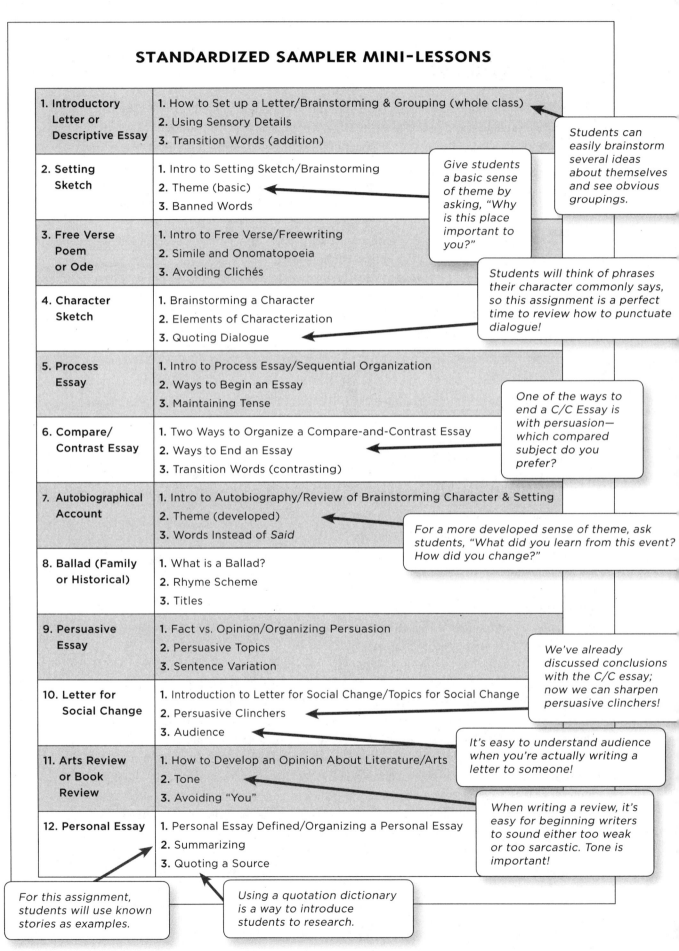

Students can easily brainstorm several ideas about themselves and see obvious groupings.

Give students a basic sense of theme by asking, "Why is this place important to you?"

Students will think of phrases their character commonly says, so this assignment is a perfect time to review how to punctuate dialogue!

One of the ways to end a C/C Essay is with persuasion—which compared subject do you prefer?

For a more developed sense of theme, ask students, "What did you learn from this event? How did you change?"

We've already discussed conclusions with the C/C essay; now we can sharpen persuasive clinchers!

It's easy to understand audience when you're actually writing a letter to someone!

When writing a review, it's easy for beginning writers to sound either too weak or too sarcastic. Tone is important!

For this assignment, students will use known stories as examples.

Using a quotation dictionary is a way to introduce students to research.

Writing Workshop in Middle School © 2013 by Marilyn Pryle • Scholastic

Ten Essential Mini-Lessons

In my experience, the ten mini-lessons listed below are the most helpful ones to teach early on so you can reinforce them the rest of the year. Of course, they don't have to be taught all at once, as you will have other specific content-related mini-lessons to teach as well. These can be taught as part of almost any assignment.

- **Brainstorming/Grouping:** Students brainstorm and then group similar thoughts together in order to form paragraphs.

- **Banned Words:** Outlaw overused words such as *good*, *bad*, and *things* for the year (see description on pages 30 and 31).

- **Sensory Details:** Students practice finding real-life details based on the five senses.

- **Transition Words:** Introduce groups of transition words (addition, sequence, contrast, and consequence)—this could be done in four separate mini-lessons.

- **Introductions (Essay):** Students discuss attention-grabbing techniques (detail, question, "Imagine . . . ," general statement, and so on) for beginning essays.

- **Avoiding *You*:** Students should avoid using the second-person tense; demonstrate ways to avoid and reword.

- **Sentence Variation:** Demonstrate ways to vary sentences; students should not begin sentences the same way in any given paragraph.

- **Theme:** Why is this essay/story/poem important? Why should the reader care? What has the main character learned? Why is the essay topic important? Demonstrate ways to communicate this.

- **Avoiding Clichés:** A sequel to the Banned Words mini-lesson, this mini-lesson outlaws all clichés. Most students need an explanation of what a cliché actually is; they don't realize they use them!

- **Maintaining the Same Tense:** In every essay/story/poem, the same tense should be maintained throughout, unless the writer purposefully chooses not to (as in a flashback).

A Note on Mini-Lessons and Pacing

In my class, students never have to wait for a certain mini-lesson to be taught in order to begin or continue a writing assignment. In fact, many mini-lessons work better when a student has writing to work with. For example, practicing how to write an introduction works best if students have already written a beginning for a piece and can now evaluate its effectiveness and rewrite it. Some students work on pace with the mini-lessons, some are ahead, and some are behind. The mini-lesson time is a wonderful way to begin class. It reminds both students and me that we are a community of writers working together, and that many writers have come before us and left a well-stocked toolbox. Every mini-lesson tells students: *You are not alone. You are not expected to know everything.* During each mini-lesson, I reach into the sturdy box of what writers know and hand students another tool to take to the shop.

Try It!

Return to the planning page, which you began during the last chapter. Using the Possible Mini-Lessons chart on page 34, add mini-lessons to the genre assignments you have chosen so far.

Make a Plan, But Be Flexible

How to Start Small

Map out mini-lessons for two assignments, and see how that goes!

As with all plans, flexibility is required. You might change assignments or mini-lessons in the middle of the year; you might cut or add; you might be inspired with a new assignment that comes to you midway through eating your sandwich at lunch or before falling asleep or while brushing your teeth. Spontaneous deviations can be the most enjoyable part of the trip. But deviations—out of spontaneity or necessity—cannot occur if the trip has not been mapped. Planning steps so that students learn in a deliberate, manageable way while still allowing for creativity and individualism will build confidence and skills simultaneously. Always keep your eye on the destination, remembering that although we plan, the destination is not a certain number of assignments or mini-lessons, or a score on a test. Rather, it is the ever-moving swirl of answers surrounding this question: "How can each of my students grow into a more independent, thoughtful, purposeful, and genuine thinker and writer in the time that we have together?"

Don't be afraid to change your plans as you see fit. Make the best choices you can now, and then trust your own judgment as the year goes on. Any effort you make with the foregoing goal in mind will help your students, even if you change the course of your journey.

Writing Workshop in Middle School © 2013 by Marilyn Pryle • Scholastic

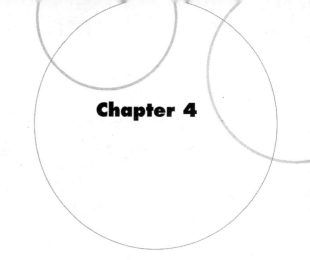

Chapter 4

Anatomy of an Assignment

Students should understand that any well-wrought piece of writing has gone through many stages. One way to reinforce this idea throughout the year is by connecting the writing process to their favorite books and movies. Emphasize to your students that these stories underwent several drafts and revisions before becoming the finished products they love.

This applies to students' writing in the workshop, too, as they draft and revise their own work. Regardless of genre, students progress through the same writing process with every assignment. This routine will create not only a sense of confidence (whatever challenges a genre may present, the writing process will lead to success) but also a sense of habit or practice. Hopefully, students will learn to enjoy not just the finished product but also the evolution of their ideas.

The Writing Process
1. Reading
2. Prewriting
3. Drafting
4. Revising
5. Editing

An assignment consists of the following parts, which spiral around the writing process:

Assignment Sheet

The assignment sheet is the map for any assignment and is usually the students' first encounter with an assignment. The top two-thirds of the sheet give step-by-step instructions about how to proceed. These steps are clearly delineated, and students check off each one as they complete it. The bottom third contains the rubric for the assignment (for more on setting up the rubrics, see Chapter 7.) At the right is a sample assignment sheet for the introductory letter.

Notice that this assignment is designated #1. For clarity, I number every assignment throughout the year. Each time students begin a new assignment, the first action they must take is to put their name on the top of the assignment sheet. I do this because I see the assignment sheet

Name _____ Date _____ Period_____

ASSIGNMENT #1

Introductory Letter

☐ Read the letter I have written to you. You are going to write a letter back to me. Follow these steps:

☐ On a sheet of paper, brainstorm any ideas about yourself that you want me to know. Be specific.

☐ Organize the information into groups. You should be putting together ideas for 3 or 4 paragraphs.

☐ Number the groups in the order that seems best.

☐ Write a first draft. Be sure to use a letter format (see my example) that includes **a recipient address, a sender's address, and a date! Don't forget to double space!**

☐ Read and revise your letter—look for places where you can add some description (sights, sounds, smells, textures, and so on).

☐ Type up the draft at your assigned computer. Remember to use the 12-point Times New Roman font; your paragraphs should be double-spaced, using the default margins and filling one page. When you are done, print your letter.

☐ Complete the Editing/Revising Checklist. Revise again and print.

☐ Submit a final draft (place it in the bin on my desk) with your brainstorming, rough drafts, Editing/Revising Checklist, and this grading sheet.

ASSIGNMENT RUBRIC	PRELIMINARY GRADE	REVISED GRADE
Structure (letter format, paragraphs, length, font) 20 pts.		
Process (brainstorm/group, draft, Editing/Revising Checklist) 20 pts.		
Description (details, examples, no banned words) 20 pts.		
Spelling 20 pts.		
Grammar (punctuation, capitals, sentences) 20 pts.		
TOTAL		

as a contract of sorts, one that clearly lists the steps involved, which the rubric reflects. Thus, the sheet makes the implicit promise that you, the teacher, are promising to grade students on what you are asking them to do. By signing their name on the sheet, students take responsibility for the assignment and thus commit to working through the steps, checking them off as they go. I do realize that students are more or less obliged to comply with the teacher, but there is still an element of trust involved. Students must trust that you will make the assignment manageable and grade them fairly, and you must trust that they will try their best to complete the assignment according to the parameters you've laid out.

Introducing the Assignment Sheet

The following is an example of how I introduce the first assignment sheet to students.

Ms. P.: At this point you've read my introductory letter to you, and your assignment now is to write a letter back to me introducing yourselves. We've practiced brainstorming and grouping ideas and talked about how to turn each group into its own paragraph. Here is the assignment sheet for this first assignment.

Joe: What are all the boxes?

Ms. P.: Each box lists a step you have to complete. Look at the first step: "Read the letter I have written to you." We've already done that. You can check it off.

Joe: Yesssss! One down.

Ms. P.: You'll start today with the second box, and just keep going through the steps in sequence at your own speed. But before you start, look at the rubric at the bottom of the assignment sheet. This shows how you'll eventually be graded. See anything you recognize?

Laura: Spelling and grammar?

Ms. P.: Good, yes, you'll have to keep an eye on grammar and spelling. What else?

Bobby: Brainstorm/group? Where it says "Process."

Ms. P.: Yes—we just talked about those, right? You'll get points for brainstorming and grouping the ideas in your letter. For every step that you do, you'll get points. Don't worry about whether the steps have a correct answer—just complete each step as best as you can, and hand in every piece of paper that goes along with the assignment, and it all gets counted.

Bryan: So even if our brainstorm is bad, and we cross parts out and write all over it, we still get points?

Ms. P.: Yes! Yes, of course! That's the best kind of brainstorm! It shows that you're thinking and revising already. That's what writers do. Just be sure to hand in everything. So, do you see how each step at the top reappears somehow in the rubric on the bottom? Good. Here's my promise to you: I'll never put anything in the rubric that we haven't discussed in class—except for the Spelling and

Grammar sections. And I'll help you with those so you can get full points in them. Anyone notice anything else interesting in the rubric?

Mollie: Is it that there are two columns? Are we doing everything twice?

Ms. P.: Not exactly. What's the second column called, Mollie?

Mollie: "Revised Grade." Oh, we get points for revising?

Ms. P.: Yes. You can revise each assignment to reach a grade of a 100. I'll help you, but you have to do the work and follow each step. But it's possible for everyone to get full points on every assignment. Does that sound fair?

A sample assignment sheet for a compare-and-contrast essay—an assignment I usually do later in the first quarter—appears below. As you can see, both in the steps and in the rubric, more is required for this assignment than for the Introductory Letter assignment—that's because by now, more has been taught in the mini-lessons.

To avoid having the assignment sheet overwhelm your students, do your best to fit the steps and rubric on a single page. As the year progresses, I include the questions for the sample reading on the photocopy of the readings themselves, which saves space on the assignment sheet.

My students usually see the compare-and-contrast essay in the earlier part of the year, before we begin persuasive text, but after we have tried a few other genres and a descriptive essay or two. Thus, students have by now had experience brainstorming, grouping, avoiding banned words and clichés, creating introductions, and using some transition words. The rubric reflects these previously learned skills, and some are highlighted in the steps of the assignment. In the mini-lessons for this assignment, I might teach the concepts of specialized organizational techniques for a compare-and-contrast piece (by subject or by characteristic), additional transition words, and ways to conclude an essay.

Teaching Tip

For an ELL class, number each checkbox so you can discuss each step as a group.

Name _____ Date _____ Period_____

ASSIGNMENT #7

Compare-and-Contrast Essay

☐ Read the two sample essays. On a sheet of paper, answer the following questions for each essay:
1. What organizational technique did the writer use?
2. What technique did the writer use for an introduction?
3. What technique did the writer use for a conclusion?
4. List three transition words in the piece.

☐ Choose two topics (people, places, objects, animals, sports, and so on) to compare and contrast. Choose topics you are interested in and know a lot about. Look through your list of "Topics for Writing" for help.

☐ On a sheet of paper, prewrite your ideas:
1. Brainstorm a list for each topic.
2. Decide which organizational technique you will use.
3. Group your ideas into paragraphs.

☐ Write a first draft. Review your notes for introduction and conclusion techniques.

☐ Revise the draft. Check for:

_____ A title   _____ An attention-grabbing introduction

_____ A strong conclusion   _____ At least four transition words

☐ Type the draft, if you have not already done so. The final copy should be at least 1 typed page.

☐ Complete the Editing/Revising Checklist and print out a final copy. Hand in everything.

ASSIGNMENT RUBRIC	PRELIMINARY GRADE	REVISED GRADE
Structure (organization, paragraphs, length, font) 20 pts.		
Process (questions, brainstorm/group, draft, Editing/Revising Checklist) 20 pts.		
Description (introduction, conclusion, banned/cliché, transition words) 20 pts.		
Spelling 20 pts.		
Grammar (punctuation, capitals, sentences) 20 pts.		
TOTAL		

Step #1 of the Writing Process: Reading

The first task of each assignment sheet is to read an example of finished work in the genre. We want students to see the connection between reading and writing. Writers do not work in a vacuum; they are avid readers who have studied and learned from writers past. I once heard the poet Ted Kooser say that he instructs his students to read 100 poems for every poem they try to write. Although this might not be possible in the middle school classroom, we can certainly illustrate the importance of reading by providing a few models with each assignment. If you had unlimited time and a complete library in your room, students could browse to their heart's fill and peruse all genres at their leisure. Since this is not the case, you must efficiently supply them with accessible but definitive examples of the genre at hand.

> The first step of the writing process is not *prewriting* but *reading*.

Include two pieces of sample reading with each assignment, and write three or four questions to accompany each. Although content and technique are deeply intertwined, these questions should focus on technique more than content. Since content is often shaped by technique, and technique can only be executed with content, the two are largely inseparable. Design your questions to reinforce whatever you have presented thus far in your mini-lessons. Having students answer the questions on a separate sheet of paper and attaching this to the rubric also ensures that they will actually read the samples.

> **Teaching Tip**
>
> Tell students that completing the sample reading questions is an easy way to get points before they've even written anything!

My genre examples come from a variety of sources. Here are some ideas about how to build up your sample reading collection:

- Get in the habit of always thinking as a teacher when you read—often in the middle of reading a novel or an op-ed piece I will think, "Good character sketch!" or "Nice conclusion!" Effective writing is out there—when you find it, throw a sticky note on the page or make a quick copy.

- Always make extra copies (or ask the student to print two copies) of student writing that could be of use in the future. Look for writing that is not only effective and polished but also illustrative of the mini-lessons.

- Use one student piece and one published piece from an experienced writer—this gives students two levels of writing to think about.

- Write your own sample, customizing your model to match your mini-lessons. This option is wonderful for two reasons: First, by revealing your own writing to students, you build a sense of trust and community in the classroom. You also get to experience what your students go through when they write the assignment. As a bonus, you could show them your prewriting and draft(s) as a model for process and revision! Writing your own sample also enables you to ensure that your mini-lesson material is reflected in the sample reading.

What you use for sample reading depends on the genre and what you have available that best serves your purposes. With certain assignments, such as the introductory letter, the only sample is an actual letter that I write to students. For the children's book, I have students root through boxes of books in the classroom and analyze three or four of their own choosing. Each assignment is different. What remains the same is that students examine a finished model of what they will write, and hopefully they gain understanding and inspiration from that model.

Below is an example of two essays that I have used as sample reading for the compare-and-contrast essay. The first is from a student in an intermediate ELL class; the second is from an advanced student in a regular eighth-grade class.

Shopping Choices

(by an ELL student)

When shopping, do you look for a comfortable setting or the lowest price? In Haiti, in the town I grew up, there are two different supermarkets. I often went to them. Their names are Delimart Super Market and Value Market. Each market has a different atmosphere, and many people always go to both places.

First, Delimart is a large shopping area with lots of parking. Many people go there, because they can find anything they need. It has automatic doors and large windows, so the inside is bright. It is comfortable because the sections are spread out and there is room to browse. The sections are separated by the type of item for sale. For example, there is one part for food, one for cosmetics, one for school supplies, one for house supplies, and one section of special wines to drink. Delimart also has a restaurant inside it.

Value Market, on the other hand, is a small market. It has some of the same items as Delimart, and it has sections for specific items. However, it often feels crowded because the aisles are smaller. The parking lot is much smaller too. In addition, Value Market does not have a restaurant. One positive quality it does have is a fresh fruit section with lots of fresh watermelon, apples, bananas and mangos.

I prefer Value Market because it is cheaper to shop there. Even though Value is not as spacious as Delimart, I can save more money there. If I save enough money at Value Market, I can eat in the restaurant with friends at Delimart!

What's Wrong with Braintree's Park?

(by an eighth-grade student)

The roar of wheels and slap of skateboards are familiar sounds at any skate park. But are all skate parks the same? To the untrained eye, Skaters Island in Rhode Island and the Braintree Skate Park near our high school may seem very similar. In reality, drastic differences leave Braintree's skate park struggling and Skaters Island prospering.

The atmospheres of both parks are extremely different. Skaters Island is a massive, 25,000 square-foot indoor skate park. It has a smooth linoleum-like floor, and Skatelite™ ramps. Braintree's park, however, is a badly designed outdoor concrete and asphalt

 Writing Workshop in Middle School © 2013 by Marilyn Pryle • Scholastic

skate park. Skaters Island has music playing at all times, giving you something to skate to, to keep your adrenaline flowing. There are colorful banners on the walls as well. Braintree Skate Park has almost the exact opposite. It is full of bland gray concrete ramps on a black asphalt round. Even on the most crowded days, it feels devoid of life.

The features of the parks differ as well. Skaters Island has a huge, flowing, wooden bowl, and an insane halfpipe. There is also a snake run. It is very well designed; you can get speed, and maintain it, something very rare in other skate parks' ramps. It has flowing hips, tight turns, and high banks, all perfect for carving. Braintree's park, on the other hand, is almost the complete opposite. The ramps have tight transition, robbing speed from the skater. The designers forgot the most important aspect of a skate park: flow. It is almost impossible to get speed anywhere in the park without vigorous pushing. And while Skaters Island has almost 40 ramps, Braintree's park has a mere nine ramps, two of which shouldn't even be counted as ramps since they are small concrete bumps.

The only characteristic where the Braintree Skate Park surpasses Skaters Island is in the people who frequent the park. I know the people at Braintree's park like friends, since I see them so often. They help and encourage me, and I do the same for them. By contrast, Skaters Island has an unknown, mysterious, sometimes ornery crowd. In addition, it is sometimes very crowded. I could stand at the lip of a bowl for 15 minutes, waiting for my 2 minute run.

Skaters Island is by far the better skate park. It was made by skaters, for skaters. Although it costs thirteen dollars for admission, it is well worth it. Braintree Skate Park is sloppily put together. The designers missed what a skate park should be. Instead of making an innovative creative outlet for skaters, they made what they, a group of non-skaters, thought would be a sufficient park.

Step #2 of the Writing Process: Prewriting

For prewriting, the next step on the assignment sheet, you can ask students to brainstorm and group ideas, freewrite, create a web or diagram, or conduct a prewrite of their choice. At the beginning of the workshop, you could do a formal lesson on brainstorming and grouping ideas using the introductory letter. With our first poem, I teach a mini-lesson on freewriting. During the compare-and-contrast essay, I show students how a Venn diagram works. In this way, I try to expose students to different methods of prewriting, many of which they have learned in their elementary years. If an assignment asks students to do a prewrite, I tell them to do whatever they are comfortable with.

Instead of, or in addition to, prewriting, you might want to have students complete a prewriting sheet. The prewriting sheet is a separate sheet that directs students more explicitly and thoroughly in the prewriting stage. You can create these yourself, highlighting any techniques you will present in the mini-lessons for the assignment or any past mini-lessons. This works for genre assignments that are more complex, or when the mini-lessons

Mini-Lesson Idea

If your students are unfamiliar with different types of *prewriting* techniques, demonstrate various methods in mini-lessons.

ASSIGNMENT #3

Ode Prewriting Sheet

Choose an object for your ode. It could be a special gift, an everyday item, something in nature, an abstract idea, and so on. It could be outside or inside, big or small—anything. It should be an object, not a person or place.

Topic: _____

Spend a few minutes thinking about your topic, then fill out the chart below. This will be your brainstorming.

Sights (shape, size, characteristics, and so on)	Colors Smells
Touch (textures, temperature)	Sounds
Personification	Onomatopoeia (look above at "Sounds")
Similes (a comparison using *like* or *as*)	Metaphor
Memories (Use the past tense.)	Why did you choose this topic? Why is it important to you?

ASSIGNMENT #8

Personal Essay Prewriting Sheet

1. What is the topic of your essay? _____

2. Write a definition of your topic (either in your own words or from a dictionary).

3. Write your personal feelings or opinions about your topic. Is it good? Bad? Useful? Important? Easy? Difficult? Common? Rare? What do you want to say about it? Brainstorm some ideas:

4. Think of one or two real-life stories that illustrate your topic and your feelings or opinions about it. For example, if you're writing about the dangers of anger, you could tell about a time when you (or someone) got angry and lost a friendship or something else important. This should be a true story from your life.

5. Look up a quote related to your topic. Copy it here, along with the author's name. You can have more than one.

6. Think about examples from books, short stories, poems, movies, etc., that illustrate your topic, and add them.

7. What's your conclusion about your topic?

8. What is an interesting way to start this essay? Write a first sentence below.

On a piece of paper, take these ideas and group them in an order that seems right to you.

contain a lot of new information. For example, I create a prewriting sheet when teaching the Ode assignment. Students are expected to use sensory details in their odes, a technique they would have learned in earlier assignments such as setting and character sketches. By the time I present the ode, we have usually discussed the idea of theme, or "why this piece is important." Finally, during the Ode assignment, I teach at least one mini-lesson on figurative language. If I simply instructed students to "freewrite about your topic and use figurative language and sensory details," I probably wouldn't get much in return. But with an explicit prewriting sheet, students brainstorm for ideas in smaller, more manageable chunks, and ultimately they come up with better poems.

Like the assignments and mini-lessons, prewriting sheets also become more developed and complex as the year goes on, reflecting all that students have learned. For example, when I have students write a basic persuasive essay in the first semester, I usually only have a step for brainstorming reasons for their opinions and grouping those reasons into paragraphs. However, later in the year, when students do a personal essay, I provide a prewriting sheet. My version of the personal essay requires students not only to formulate an opinion on a topic, but also to support that

Teaching Tip

Differentiate instruction by creating two or more versions of a prewriting sheet—one with more structure and guidance for struggling students, and one with more advanced requirements for students who need a bigger challenge.

opinion with snippets of autobiography, literature, popular culture, and a bit of research. Explaining the process on the assignment sheet would be adequate for some students, but providing a prewriting sheet is much more effective for everyone.

Notice that both prewriting sheets shown include spaces for brainstorming; tell students to use additional paper to brainstorm or web as much as they like. Note, too, that at the bottom of a personal essay prewriting sheet students must assimilate and group their ideas on a separate piece of paper. Some of the really complex assignments, such as the short story analysis or the analysis of a poem, have prewriting sheets that cover two sides of a page. The more information I can get students to summon before writing, the more information will make it into their papers.

How To Design a Prewriting Sheet

1. List the components of the genre assignment. For example, does the assignment require students to provide reasons or examples? Sensory details? A strong introduction and conclusion? List the assignment's parts.

2. Make a list of the concepts you will teach in the accompanying mini-lessons. Add concepts you have taught in previous mini-lessons.

3. Look at your lists of what you want the students to do. Think about how you can visually organize these concepts so students can add their own thoughts without feeling overwhelmed. For example, consider the following:

- a chart or web, with space for students to add their ideas
- a flowchart to show a sequence of ideas
- a storyboard
- a series of questions, with space for students to answer
- a two-part prewriting sheet, with a chart at the top of the page and some questions below

4. Design the prewriting sheet so the information is manageable for students.

The main goal of a teacher-generated prewriting sheet is to break down the components of a writing assignment into small chunks. This way, students can think of ideas in an organized manner without feeling overwhelmed by the overall task.

I stress to students that with all prewriting, they are in control of what they decide to use or not. The purpose of prewriting is to stir the brain and see what bubbles up. They don't have to include it all in their drafts, and they can always add new ideas later. They are in charge. The only "wrong" way to do prewriting is not to try.

Often, the last idea of a prewrite will be the one that gives birth to the piece. I tell students that this happens regularly and that they should never view the time spent prewriting all the other ideas as a waste. Rather, they should see those ideas as the winding path to the usable idea. I invite them to use as many pages or prewriting sheets as they need and to save the old stuff, even if it seems "bad." And then I tell them there is no such thing as a "bad" idea, only ideas that are either usable or unusable in the moment.

Step #3 in the Writing Process: Drafting

The next step on the assignment sheet is the first draft. I let students choose if they wish to write their first drafts by hand or type them on the computer. They should have their prewriting in clear view and then simply begin writing. Most students are able to do this, but some, even with a full prewrite, are still unable to start. I give students the following piece of advice that usually works: *start badly on purpose*. The conversation usually goes something like this:

Ms. P.: Emily, I see that you have a lot of ideas in your brainstorming, but you're staring at your paper. What's the problem?

Emily: I know what I want to write, I just don't know where to start.

Ms. P.: How about with one of your sensory details—a color, or a sound? I see some listed on your prewriting sheet. You can't go wrong with a detail in your first sentence.

Emily: I know . . . I just don't know which one. I just can't decide.

Ms. P.: Try this: Give yourself permission to start badly. Actually, why don't you try starting badly on purpose? Write two sentences that are deliberately bad and then just keep going. We'll change them later.

Emily: Really? Just start by saying something like, "This is a story about . . ."

Ms. P.: Yes. Two or three sentences you know are bad. Then keep going.

Emily: OK . . . I didn't know we were allowed to do that!

I again remind students that while writing, they can add or delete ideas from their prewriting; they should not feel trapped by it. Sometimes students even begin a new piece of prewriting after they've written a few sentences and realized they want to write about something else. This is what writers do!

Step #4 in the Writing Process: Revising

After students have written or typed a first draft, they should revise it in a different-colored pen so the new ideas are visible. (I keep pens of several different colors in the room.) On the assignment sheet, I usually give a short list of reminders of what to look for when revising. These reminders always reflect new and recent mini-lessons. After writing in their revisions, students should type them in (or type the entire paper if they have not yet done so) and print the piece again. Of course, they are welcome to generate

Writing Workshop in Middle School © 2013 by Marilyn Pryle • Scholastic

as many drafts as they want; the minimum is two. All drafts get handed in with the rest of the work, and students get points for drafting and revising in the Process section of the rubric.

Encourage your students to skip lines as they write and type double-spaced so there is room to write on the page and in between the words. It may seem obvious, but if you don't repeat this directive, students will not do it.

When students are satisfied with a solid draft, they must complete an Editing/Revising Checklist and make one more set of changes. The questions on this sheet give reminders about what students should have looked for in revising and lead them to the editing process.

Step #5 in the Writing Process: Editing (and some continued revising)

To help students edit (and revise a bit more), I use an Editing/Revising Checklist. I keep a pile of these sheets in the room at all times so students can use one when they are ready. The sheet consists of a series of questions directing students to reexamine the content, writing techniques, and conventions they've used in their papers.

Throughout the year, I move students through four versions of the E/R Checklist, one for each quarter. I do this for two reasons. First, if I do not modify the checklist, students quickly become familiar with it and begin checking off the answers to questions mindlessly. Introducing a new version each quarter forces them to think about the questions. But secondly, and more important, with each new checklist, I try to nudge students toward greater autonomy. Every new E/R Checklist gives less explicit instruction than the last and requires students to self-check more. Additionally, each checklist incorporates the technical mini-lessons taught during that particular quarter. E/R Checklists appear on pages 153–156.

E/R Checklist #1: The first E/R Checklist is a brief, nonthreatening list of yes/no questions that directs students to confirm whether or not they have included a deliberate introduction and conclusion, paragraphs, and transition words. It also asks them to check for banned words and clichés, to examine commas and capitals, and to use the spell-checker program.

Editing/Revising Checklist 1

Read your draft. Then answer the questions below to help you revise.

	YES	NEED TO REVISE
1. Do I have an introduction?		
2. Does each paragraph contain **one main idea** with examples?		
3. Do I have a conclusion?		
4. Do I **avoid** banned words such as *good, bad, cool, stuff,* and *things*?		
5. Do I avoid clichés?		
6. Do I **try** to use transition words like *however, although, moreover, consequently,* and *in addition to*?		
7. Did I use the spell-checker?		
8. Did I check all commas? (Should they be periods?)		
9. Did I capitalize all proper names and titles?		

Writing Workshop in Middle School by Marilyn Pryle • Scholastic 153

E/R Checklist #2: The second E/R Checklist focuses on many of the same topics, but does not use the yes/no format. Instead, students must think more specifically; for example, rather than simply checking for an introduction, students must identify the chosen method for the introduction. Similarly, students must identify their method or methods of concluding. (At first, students answer these introduction and conclusion questions by circling a method from a list; in the third quarter, a list is given.) Likewise, instead of simply checking for banned words and clichés, students must ask themselves which ones seem to recur in their writing. New concepts on the second-quarter E/R Checklist include changing weak verbs, varying sentence lengths, and checking for homophones.

Editing/Revising Checklist 2

Read your draft. Use the questions below to help you revise.

1. What kind of introduction do I have? (*Circle one.*)

   Question   Imagine . . .   Interesting fact   Quote

   Sensory detail *(sight, sound, smell, taste, touch)*

   Other (describe) _____

2. What is in my conclusion? (*Circle any that apply.*)

   Summary of ideas   Theme or message   Solution to a problem

   Opinion   Frame with introduction

   Other (describe) _____

3. Do I use any banned words or clichés? If so, replace them. What is one banned word I use often? _____

4. Do I include at least three transition words? _____

5. Do I use weak verbs? If so, replace some. _____

6. Are my sentences varied? Are they different lengths with different beginnings? _____

7. Find one flat sentence and change it.

8. Did I use the spell-checker? _____

9. Did I look up any unfamiliar homophones? _____ Name one: _____

10. Check all commas. Should I change any to periods? _____

11. What is one special problem I should check for in my writing? (Write it below and check for it.)

    _____

Editing/Revising Checklist 3

Read your draft. Use the questions below to help you revise.

1. What technique did I use for my introduction? _____

2. What technique did I use for my conclusion? _____

3. How is my organization? Describe it: _____

   _____

4. Language: Banned words? _____   Weak verbs? _____

5. Do I have sentence variation? _____ Transition words? _____

6. What is my tone for this piece? _____

   Is it appropriate for my audience? _____

7. Did I use the spell-checker? _____

8. Are all my verbs in the same tense? _____

9. What is one punctuation rule I should check for? Check for it.

   _____

10. What are two problems I should check for in my writing?

    • _____

    • _____

    Check for them.

Finally, and significantly, the last question on this checklist asks students to identify one special problem to check for in their writing. This guides students to recognize their own habits as writers.

E/R Checklist #3: The third-quarter E/R Checklist requires students to think just as closely about their work but also to supply more of the information themselves. So, instead of circling methods of writing introductions and conclusions from a list, they must write the chosen method in the blanks provided. This pushes students to both classify and remember the techniques they have learned thus far. The third question on the checklist asks students to describe the organization of the piece, again forcing them to analyze and classify their own writing. In addition, these questions communicate to students that they should be making deliberate choices as they write. My goal is to change their thinking gradually with each assignment. By constantly focusing and refocusing on these topics, I hope that students will come to view themselves as deliberate crafters of their writing. New questions on the third checklist deal with tone and verb tense. At the end, I ask students to check for one punctuation rule (they can choose) and two "special problems."

E/R Checklist #4: The last checklist of the year only gives four categories (Structure and Organization, Description and Language, Grammar and Spelling, and Special Problems) and asks students to come up with their own areas within each category to check. They must remember two or three areas per category, fill these areas in the blanks provided, and check a box to show they have evaluated their paper in that area. Of course, they can (and should) use the areas we practiced all year, like introductions, avoiding clichés, looking for fragments, and so on. Thus, students must be self-sufficient in remembering what exactly to look for when they revise and edit their papers; I give only the categories. In addition, they must be particularly aware of which pitfalls most often snag them individually. It is my hope that when they have left my class, or when they are taking a test on their own, they will remember the categories and self-check. (I sometimes give them acronyms like "LOG," which stands for Language, Organization, and Grammar.) So, at the end of the year, we have come full circle: as with the first checklist, students must check off yes/no-type questions; however, instead of my supplying and controlling all of the information, they must demonstrate what they have internalized.

Editing/Revising Checklist 4

Read your draft. Use the questions below to help you revise.

Structure and Organization: List three areas you should always check, and check them:

Areas	Checked
1. _____	☐
2. _____	☐
3. _____	☐

Description and Language: List three areas and check them:

Areas	Checked
1. _____	☐
2. _____	☐
3. _____	☐

Grammar and Spelling: List three areas and check them:

Areas	Checked
1. _____	☐
2. _____	☐
3. _____	☐

Special Problems: List two problem areas that you have been working on this year:

Areas	Checked
1. _____	☐
2. _____	☐

Writing Workshop in Middle School by Marilyn Pryle • Scholastic 156

At the beginning of the year, teach a mini-lesson to explain the concept of the E/R Checklist and to introduce the first one. Mention that it will change each quarter, but you don't need to go into too much detail. Instead, take a few minutes at the beginning of each new quarter to introduce the corresponding E/R Checklist and point out some differences. Since the changes are gradual, students feel prepared; you can also emphasize that there are no "right" or "wrong" answers, only degrees of effort in self-analysis. And, since the E/R Checklist is factored into every rubric under the Process category, students will be conscientious about its completion.

Cross-Curricular Idea!

Give versions of the E/R Checklists to teachers of other subjects so they can use them with their own writing assignments (big or small).

When students have completed an assignment, they gather the following and hand it in as a package:

- answers to the sample reading questions
- second draft
- prewriting
- E/R Checklist
- first draft
- Assignment Sheet

Since all students work at their own pace, they will not hand in each assignment at the same time. After handing in an assignment, they should begin the next one. In the meantime, I take home finished papers handed in that day and read them.

Rubric

As mentioned earlier, a rubric appears at the bottom of every Assignment Sheet. Since a rubric is part of the assignment sheet, students always know beforehand what they will be graded on and how these expectations match the instructions. A full explanation of the rubric can be found in Chapter 7.

How to Create an Assignment Sheet

1. Always leave a space at the top for the student's name and the date.

2. Fill in the assignment number and name.

3. Use checkboxes or circles so students can check off a completed task.

4. Give a task for the sample reading. Type questions on the assignment sheet or, if there is not enough room, type them on the sample reading.

5. Give tasks in sequence for the following:

   - **Topic:** Show students how to search for and choose a topic.

   - **Prewriting:** You may want to break this down into micro-tasks.

   - **Drafting:** You can remind students of something they've learned (such as paragraphs, introductions, or skipping lines).

   - **Revising:** List specifically what students should look for. Base your list on what you have taught so far in mini-lessons. You can use lines or circles so students can check off these micro-tasks.

   - **Typing:** Remind students of the minimum length.

   - **Editing/Revising Checklist:** Remind students about handing in everything together.

(Note: These tasks above can be divided or combined, depending on the amount of work for each one. For example, on the Introductory Letter assignment on page 42, I used three checkboxes for the prewriting phase, which is a main focus of the assignment.)

Writing Workshop in Middle School © 2013 by Marilyn Pryle • Scholastic

Try It!

If you are ready, try making an assignment sheet for the first assignment you chose in your planning page. See the steps on the previous page for creating an assignment sheet—take a few minutes to draft the instructions for your first assignment.

Correcting/Revising (Based on My Grading)

After I read a paper, I write suggestions on it (both specific and general, depending on the level of work), and give it a preliminary grade, I return it to the student for another revision. (On pages 100 and 101 I discuss in detail how I correct a paper.) During this stage, I try to meet with each student at least once to explain my remarks and assist in revising. Students then incorporate the changes and resubmit the paper for points back. This stage can be repeated many times: After a student has revised the work based on my notes, I revise the grades in the rubric. However, if students want to revise again or missed some of my suggestions the first time, they can do that and hand in the paper once more. I will then check the newest revision and again change the grade.

It's worth emphasizing that even as students are revising and handing in a paper several times, they can begin (and maybe even finish) a new assignment at the same time. The revising stage always overlaps with new work. With so many papers to read and students to visit, one cannot possibly produce immediate feedback! Students should understand that when they hand in one paper, they should go on to the next assignment.

> **Student Note**
>
> "Getting points back gives you the courage to try harder the second time around."
>
> —Malorie M.

Spelling Practice Sheet

If students misspell a word, I have them write the word correctly five times on a Spelling Practice Sheet. I tell students that with the existence of spell-checking today, there is really little excuse for misspelled words. There are exceptions, of course, like homophones. It is helpful to do a mini-lesson on homophones at some point in the year, and I hang teaching posters about them in the room. If a paper still makes it to my desk with misspellings, then the student must practice

Spelling Practice Sheet

Write each misspelled word five times.
Hand in this sheet with your revised assignment.

1. _____   1. _____
2. _____   2. _____
3. _____   3. _____
4. _____   4. _____
5. _____   5. _____

1. _____   1. _____
2. _____   2. _____
3. _____   3. _____
4. _____   4. _____
5. _____   5. _____

1. _____   1. _____
2. _____   2. _____
3. _____   3. _____
4. _____   4. _____
5. _____   5. _____

Writing Workshop in Middle School by Marilyn Pryle • Scholastic 157 writing the word five times. Sometimes I will write a note to the student with directions to write the word along with its definition. For example, if *its* is used in the paper for *it's*, I will have the student write "it's = it is" five times. Or, if *than* is used for *then* in an "if/then" construction, I will instruct the student to write "if . . . then . . ." five times.

This technique is very basic, but it works on two levels. First, if students are simply being lazy with spelling, they will discover that they have merely created more work for themselves. This realization does ultimately have an impact on many students. Second, and more important, many misspellings are just bad habits, and by repeating the correct habit, even if only five times, students' habits will begin to change. Many misspellings are computer-generated bad habits, such as using *defiantly* instead of *definitely*, but are still unacceptable; writing the correct word five times may inspire students to pay closer attention to what the computer is telling them to do, or doing for them. Questioning the computer is a valuable skill for an adolescent! At any rate, completion of the Spelling Practice Sheet is factored into the spelling section of the rubric.

Students Who Need More Spelling Support

Of course, this method is not intended for students who have learning disabilities that inhibit spelling. Having those students spend huge chunks of valuable time writing and rewriting words is unproductive. The same is true to an extent for ELL learners. With both of these groups, you can focus instead on patterns. For example, search for the top three frequently misspelled words throughout a paper and have the student write those. Or choose only misspelled words that have the same orthographic pattern and have the student write those. On the other hand, if a wide variety of misspellings abound throughout a paper, you can isolate a single paragraph and focus on a few words there. Each student in this category will differ according to background and ability, and what his or her learning support team may already have recommended.

Putting the Parts Together

Spend some time at the beginning of the year walking students through the first few assignments and repeating the parts and class procedures. Soon you will see students catch on and the class run smoothly by itself. The step-by-step instruction of the assignment sheets is integral to this phenomenon, but the overall supportive nature of the workshop also helps students from getting overwhelmed. For example, students always have a chance to revise their work; they cannot write a wrong answer on a brainstorm or freewrite; they can work at their own pace and ask for help with anything. They learn to trust the process of the workshop as well as the teacher. Students know they won't be penalized for honest mistakes, and they won't be publicly ridiculed for forgetting where the E/R Checklists are located. It's a safe environment, one that really is only about them and their writing. Once students realize this, they settle in to a peaceful and consistent pattern of work and self-reliance.

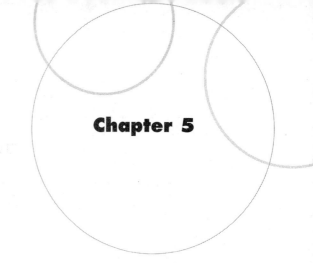

Chapter 5

Setting up the Workshop Space

Few times stress a teacher more than the weeks prior to the beginning of school. Even experienced teachers get a bit distracted and fidgety once August hits. As is true with any subject in a curriculum, the more work done beforehand, the more smoothly the class runs in real time. This is especially true in writing workshop, due to the volume of student papers to be read once the year begins.

This chapter focuses on the general running of the workshop and the ways the set-up of your physical space can help the workshop flow. As the year progresses and you become more familiar with the needs of your students, you will get your own ideas. To help you get started, here are some techniques that have worked for me.

The Classroom

My goal in setting up my room is for the space to be student-centered, not teacher-centered. I want students to feel that they have a physical and mental space in which to write and think. Most important, I know that in order for the class to run as a true workshop, students have to be comfortable working at their own pace and helping themselves to the materials they need to support their creativity and productivity. I cannot have them interrupting me every three minutes asking for a stapler or thesaurus. Ultimately, the more user-friendly I can make the room, the more quality time I have to work with students on improving their writing.

Setting up a user-friendly, student-centered environment encourages students to take ownership of their work and gives them the space to be creative. To begin, ask yourself the questions on the next page. These ideas are explained fully throughout this chapter. You might not find all of these ideas useful, but don't worry! Just let your mind work, and jot down your thoughts.

Exploring My Space

Could I place desks in a circle or horseshoe to give a writing-community feel to the room? If not, what else could I do to give a feeling of community?

How would I manage computer use? Would having a schedule or sign-up sheet be useful? Would students go to a computer lab?

Where is the best place to keep writing materials, dictionaries, thesauri, and the like so students have easy access to them?

Where is the most accessible location to keep handouts for writing assignments? How might I display the handouts so they are quickly identifiable?

What space, special chair, or stool can I set aside for students to read their work?

Where could I store extra reading material, in case students wish to read more than the sample readings in the assignments?

Where is the best place for students to store their writing notebooks?

Could I place an extra chair by my desk, or set aside space in the room, so students can approach me with questions?

Keep these questions in mind as you read the rest of this chapter.

Writing Workshop in Middle School © 2013 by Marilyn Pryle • Scholastic

Desks

If you have your own classroom and have control over the layout, consider arranging desks in a circle or horseshoe (or layered horseshoe). This can give the room that collaborative, workshop feeling, the sense that students are all working together to improve their writing. It makes mini-lessons and student readings less intimidating; it reinforces the idea that students and teacher together form a community of writers. Of course, if you share a room or simply do not have space to rearrange desks, you can create the community feeling in other ways, such as by having small-group readings of work.

I should also add that a circle or horseshoe arrangement is not a good fit for every classroom. If you feel certain that your class would not pay attention in that configuration, then hold off on it. It is more important to first get the class "on board"; people cannot write if they are distracted. Once a tone of respectful order is established, the next step can be taken toward nurturing a writing community.

Whether you are able to rearrange your room or not, always remember the most important factor in establishing a community atmosphere is your attitude and tone: If you believe in your students' abilities, and if this belief shines through in your words and expression, students will respond.

Computers

I have taught writing workshop in rooms that had a computer for every student and in rooms with no computers. In the latter case, I had students do their typing at home (or during a study hall if they had computer access) and their in-class writing and revising by hand. If you have only a few computers in your room, create a sign-up sheet or rotating schedule and combine it with the at-home method. You also might be able to work with your school librarian or computer instructor to negotiate more computer time. If there is a computer lab in the school, you might be able to schedule time for a computer day in which all students do their typing. They could do rough drafts by hand until then. Although a lack of computers may slow down the amount of writing in a workshop, it is certainly not a deal-breaker. Students can get all the benefits of writing workshop when they write in longhand.

Storing Student Work

Storage space refers to a place to put things so they are easily accessible when we need them. However, the purpose of storage goes deeper than that: when our work is kept in a neat, orderly fashion, we feel a greater sense of accomplishment when we survey it. We feel motivated to continue and are less distracted. Whole books have been written on the negative impact of clutter, so I'll simply summarize by stating that clutter is stagnant, time-wasting, and debilitating—and obviously not conducive to the flow of writing! Organizing and storing student work can be a challenge for both students and teachers. In my classroom, I aim to meet the following goals for storing student work:

> When work is ordered and neat, we feel a greater sense of accomplishment.

1. Students learn to be organized and uncluttered.

2. Students can access their work, old and new, easily and without disturbing other students.

3. Current writing assignments are kept in a secure spot.

4. Graded work can be efficiently returned to students.

5. Finished writing assignments are orderly and complete.

6. Students feel proud of their accumulation of finished work and their growth as writers.

As you read this list, you may be thinking of your own struggles and successes in managing student work. Here are some suggestions for achieving these goals.

Folders

Whether students write in class or at home, I recommend setting up two folders for each student:

- a working folder for writing in progress
- a finished folder for completed, graded pieces

If students do all their writing in class, you can store their working folders in the classroom; if they do some of their work outside the classroom, they can carry their working folders to and from class.

> **Organizing Idea**
>
> **Two Folders per Student**
> - Working Folder
>   (in-progress work)
> - Finished Folder
>   (completed, graded work)

Working Folders

Students' in-progress work can be stored in manila folders in an easily reachable place in your room. I should stress that only materials related to the current writing assignment go in this folder. The only exception is if students are working on revising an old assignment in addition to working on a new assignment, in which case all the revision material would also go into the folder. Students should only work on one new assignment at a time, and any scraps from finished assignments should not linger in the working folders. Similarly, pages from other subjects should not make their way into these folders. Even one piece of stray paper has a way of multiplying and should be removed. This simple practice in itself can be an important lesson in organization for many students.

Early in my career I stored the working folders in a crate in the back of the room, which I thought was very accessible, but at the beginning of each class, a human traffic jam formed around the crate. Naturally, this was very disruptive. Even on better days there was a long line. I realized I would have to make the working folders even more accessible, so I taped them to the walls. First, I wrote each student's name in large letters across the front of a folder. Then I stapled the sides of each folder so the front flap bowed open, making the folder permanently gape to facilitate the insertion and removal of papers. At first, I grouped working folders for each class, but realized alphabetizing all the folders was more efficient. On the first of day school, I have students locate their folders. After that, students retrieve their work from their folders as they enter the room.

If you have enough wall space, this arrangement might work for you. If you don't, there are other options. Working folders can be stored in a crate; however, as I noted above, time is lost as students wait in line for their turn at the crate. One solution is to station three or four crates at various places in the room, and instead of organizing each by class, organize all the folders alphabetically. By placing a crate in one corner of the room labeled "A–H," another crate in another corner labeled "I–P," and so on, students disperse to various crates instead of gathering around just one.

If students are working on their writing assignments outside of class, the working folder can be a pocketed folder (instead of a manila one), which students are responsible for bringing to every workshop meeting. To avoid confusion, this working folder should be kept separate from their other subjects. At any given time, this folder might hold brainstorming ideas, notes, drafts from the current assignment, or in-progress revisions.

The working folders serve students well. At the end of any given class, students might be at any stage of the writing process; they might have a single page on their desk if they are beginning an assignment, or ten if they're nearing the end. Whatever the case, at the end of class they only need to scoop up whatever is on their desk and deposit it in the folder until the next class. When students return to class, they can conveniently grab the folders as they enter the room en route to their seats.

Working folders simplify things for you as well. When I have a graded revision to give back to a student, I can simply deposit the paper in that student's folder before class. (Often, though, I like to hand the paper back personally and praise the student on work well done. But at least I have the option in case I am pressed for time.) Additionally, I can quickly return any stray papers I discover after class to their rightful place. All of these small measures will enable you to be more focused during class time, so you and your students can get down to the real business at hand: writing.

How to Start Small

If you don't have time to create and secure working folders on the wall, hand out manila folders on the first day and have students write their names on the tabs. Then ask students to store the folders in a designated spot. As the year progresses, you can continue to think about the most efficient way to store and distribute the working folders.

Finished Folders

Finished folders are for completed and graded pieces of writing. Students have completed all the assigned steps for the genre, written at least two drafts, conferenced with me at some point over the drafts, corrected the drafts, and printed a final clean copy. After helping students revise and correct a piece, I give the final grade. At this point, students do the following:

- remove the paper clip that holds all the material for the assignment and staple them together
- retrieve their finished folders
- complete the assignment log inside the front cover. A template appears on page 157.
- put the completed assignment in the finished folder and replace it in its rightful alphabetical position in the filing cabinet

Each finished folder should have an assignment log attached to the inside of it where students can record the assignment number, title of their piece, genre, and date filed. On the first day of class, have students write their names on the tabs of the finished folders and on the assignment logs, and staple them to the folders.

Since all students will not be using their finished files every day, there is no need

> **Tip**
>
> Keep a stapler near the finished folder cabinet so it is available for students when they need one.

Assignment Log

Name: Mollie S. School Year: 2009-2010

#	Date	Assignment Name	Title
1	9/10/09	Introductory Letter	Dear Ms. Pryle
2	9/18/09	Setting Sketch	My Room
3	9/29/09	Process Essay	How to Play Defense
4	10/07/09	Free Verse Poem	Dolphins
5	10/16/09	Character Sketch	Tiffany Powell, My Best Friend
6	10/26/09	Eyewitness Account	A-Rod in Scranton
7	11/04/09	Compare/Contrast Essay	Two schools
8	11/12/09	Autobiographical Essay	On the Way to Virginia Beach
9	11/23/09	Ode	Ode to My Sneakers
10	12/09/09	Persuasive Essay	Why Close Sacred Heart?
11	12/13/09	Retelling of a Legend	The Legend of Mom Murphy
12	1/11/10	Ballad	The Ballad of Babe Ruth
13	1/22/10	Letter for Social Change	Dear Senator Casey
14	2/01/10	Free Choice (Ode)	Ode to My 3-Wood
15	2/11/10	Children's Book	The Boat Ride
16	2/24/10	Analysis of a Short Story	Analysis of "Charles"
17	3/05/10	Short Story	The Pepper-Eating Contest
18	3/10/10	Free Verse Poem	Mae's Porch
19	3/22/10	Book Review	A Visit to Mango Street
20	4/21/10	Personal Essay	On Friendship
21	4/15/10	Test Writing	
22	4/30/10	Analysis of a Poem	"While I Slept" by Robert Francis
23	5/07/10	Poem in Form (Sonnet)	The Beach
24	5/18/10	Arts Review	High School Musical 3 the Best Yet
25	5/27/10	Parody	Fire And Mice
26	6/08/10	Letter of Submission for Publication	Dear Editor

Sample Assignment Log

Plan It!

Will students' working folders be kept in the room, or will students bring them to and from class?

If the working folders are stored in the room, where will you put them? Can they go in crates, in a filing cabinet, or on the walls?

Where can you store your students' finished folders? Can you keep a stapler nearby?

Draw It!

Take a minute to examine this Sample Classroom Blueprint. Use this model to help you draw the basic layout of your room—door and windows, students' desks, computer stations, and your desk. Draw potential spaces for the working folders and finished folders. Keep this blueprint handy as you read the rest of the chapter.

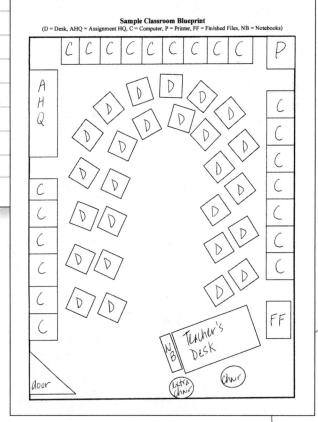

Sample Classroom Blueprint
(D = Desk, AHQ = Assignment HQ, C = Computer, P = Printer, FF = Finished Files, NB = Notebooks)

to have them accessible at any moment. You can keep them in a filing cabinet or crate, arranged by class. Within each class section, finished folders can be arranged alphabetically. During the first week of class, I thoroughly explain where students can find their finished folder. After some students have finished the first assignment, it's helpful to do a whole-class demonstration of how to file it. For most students, watching it done once is enough.

The benefits of this system are obvious. At any moment, you (or your students) can view the completed assignments, in chronological order, with final grades clearly displayed. This is especially helpful during parent conferences or if the principal or guidance counselor requests to see a particular student's file. In addition, students can easily locate a specific assignment for quick reference or to submit it for publication.

Dare I dream that this small lesson in organization will help students in other areas of their lives? Teaching them to keep things in order, to record, to label—these are life skills. Even returning a folder to its proper alphabetical position is a worthwhile exercise.

The most important lesson comes last. Students don't always sense the magnitude of their work, but by the end of the year, when they can see (and hold in their hands) the massive amount of brainstorming, drafting, and revising they've done, when they read the long list of genres they've tried, and when they acknowledge their success in the stack of final grades, they feel a strong and well-earned sense of accomplishment and growth.

Assignment Headquarters

In a workshop setting, students must learn to work autonomously. They need unfettered access to Assignment Headquarters, a place for their writing folders and other materials they may need to complete a piece of writing, such as assignment sheets, sample reading, loose-leaf paper, E/R Checklists, Spelling Practice Sheets, writing utensils, and other useful tools.

Assignment Crate

Since each assignment includes an assignment sheet, sample reading, and sometimes a prewriting sheet, think about a space in your room where these materials could go. An efficient solution is to store the materials in folders and put these in a crate. (You might also use a filing cabinet or simply designate a surface where separate folders can go.) A crate is a simple solution that takes up relatively little space. Label a hanging folder for each numbered assignment. Within it, place manila folders for a corresponding assignment sheet, sample reading, and any prewriting sheets; place one copy of the sample reading in the folder and copies for each student of the rest of the material.

Organizing Idea

Clearly label all handouts for an assignment, and place them in a self-serve crate.

You need not make copies of the sample reading for each student. Once students have examined the sample reading and answered the required questions, they can re-file this material for the next class. Instruct students to keep the sample reading and questions clean and return them to the appropriate folder. Of course, you may want students to base their writing on the sample reading—for example, you could have them analyze the rhyme and meter of a specific poem and write about it in preparation for writing their own formal poems. In this case you would make enough copies for every student. These cases are limited, however, and I am happy to save time and trees by usually photocopying a single class set.

Put this assignment crate on the opposite side of the room from your desk to spread activity around the room. Students frequently come and go from the headquarters, retrieving or replacing papers, and though they usually do this one or two at a time, they will be separate from students who come to your desk for one reason or another. Any table surface can hold the crate, or a windowsill could suffice. Try to use as much of your room as possible: spread out the filing space for finished folders, the assignment crate, and your desk (or any conferencing space) so students aren't distracted when filing a finished assignment or retrieving the thesaurus.

If your students will not be moving from assignment to assignment on their own, as in an ELL class, then you might not need an assignment crate. Let's say you're doing writing workshop once a week, and your students are all starting each assignment together and finishing it at home. In this case, you can simply keep the necessary handouts with you and hand them out en masse; there is no need to have a space for students to get the next assignment.

Loose-Leaf Paper

Make sure to keep plenty of loose-leaf paper available. It can be used for prewriting of any kind and for answering questions about the sample reading. You can keep this paper supply in a labeled folder in the back of the assignment crate or, if space permits, in a stack beside it.

Editing/Revising Checklists and Spelling Practice Sheets

Students use one Editing/Revising Checklist for each assignment, so it is worthwhile to make up a bunch at the beginning of the quarter and keep them in a designated place in your room, replenishing the pile as it thins. Also, place nearby a stack of other sheets your students will be using frequently, like Spelling Practice Sheets. Both of these sheets can be kept in the assignment crate in their own labeled folders or in another place that is easily accessible. One alternative to photocopying so many Editing/Revising Checklists is to display it on a large poster. Hang the poster, and create an Editing/Revising Station where students can go to check their work and get ideas for revision. You could even move a desk or two, or a stool, below the poster. An alternative to creating Spelling Practice Sheets is to have students rewrite spelling words on the back of their prewriting or drafts.

Paper-Saving Alternative

If you don't want to photocopy the E/R Checklist for each student, you can copy it onto a poster and have students consult it to check their work.

Writing Utensils and Other Materials

Pens, pencils, and highlighters, scissors and tape are the basic materials that you need to keep on hand for a writing workshop. It would be nice if students came to

Plan It!

Will your students be moving from assignment to assignment on their own, or will you be starting each assignment together as a group?

If students are moving through assignments on their own, where can you put all the materials for each assignment? Would an assignment crate work? Where would it go in your room?

Where can you put the Editing/Revising Checklists and Spelling Practice Sheets? Will you set them out, or will you try one of the alternatives, such as creating a poster?

Where can you put loose-leaf paper: in the assignment crate or at another location?

Where can you put pens, pencils, highlighters, tape, and scissors? Which items do you think you might want to keep at your desk?

Do you want all of these items grouped together at an Assignment Headquarters? Where would you allocate space for that in your room? If you would rather spread the items throughout the room, where would you place each one?

Writing Workshop in Middle School © 2013 by Marilyn Pryle • Scholastic

class prepared with their own pens and pencils, but as we all know, it helps to have extras on hand, and colored pens are especially useful during the revision process. At the end of class, be sure to give students enough time to return classroom materials. These can be kept near the assignment crate or another convenient location. It seems logical to keep colored pens near the Editing/Revising Checklists. You may want to keep some of these materials close to you. For example, I have resorted to keeping highlighters on my desk in order to monitor the borrowers; I have also on occasion moved the scissors to my top drawer to be used on a request-only basis.

Add It!

If you want to use an Assignment Headquarters, label it on your room blueprint. If items such as loose-leaf paper, Editing/Revising Checklists, Spelling Practice Sheets, and writing materials will be spread throughout the room, designate these spaces on the blueprint.

Other Helpful Resources

If you have space, it's helpful to keep a dictionary, almanac, thesaurus, rhyming dictionary, and grammar handbook readily available to students. Although students need not use all of these reference tools for every assignment, they should know that these books are always at their disposal, and often I will refer a student to one of these resources during an individual conference. You may also want to keep literature anthologies, classical and contemporary, books of short stories and poetry, novels, and a sampling of textbooks from other classes.

How To Start Small

Don't worry about gathering all of these books just yet—simply refer students to the Internet for now. As time goes on, you will naturally acquire a mini-library of student resources.

Handing-In Space

During my first year of facilitating the workshop, I quickly realized that having an organized, designated "handing-in" spot would lessen my grading time and give students a final ritual for each written piece that would highlight its importance and the amount of work they had done. Instead of having students leave their final drafts in a pile on my desk, I ask them to hand in every bit of work for each assignment. On my desk sits a wire bin labeled "Papers to Be Graded." I ask my students to arrange their writing in reverse chronological order, with the final piece on the top and the earliest work (the prewriting) below. Other material, such as the answers to the sample reading questions, the E/R Checklist, and Spelling Practice Sheet, go on the bottom. This seemed easy enough to remember, but after I had to repeat it about 65 times as students completed their first assignment, I was moved to make a small sign, laminate it, and affix it to my desk next to the bin designated for completed work.

> **Organizing Idea**
>
> Have a specific place where all work always gets handed in.

Handing-In Order

TOP	Assignment Sheet
	Final Copy (or Latest Revision)
	Rough Draft
	Prewriting
	Answers to Sample Reading Questions
	Editing/Revising Checklist
BOTTOM	Spelling Practice Sheet (optional)

> **Organizing Idea**
>
> Use a different colored folder for each class's ungraded work. Use stacked paper bins, one per class, to hold graded work.

This method does not differentiate between first-time hand-ins and revisions; all work gets put in the same bin. If the work is a revision, you will know that because you will see your preliminary grades written on the rubric; the revised draft should come first, with the marked-up, most recent draft right under it. This way, you can easily flip between the two drafts to see if the recommended changes were incorporated.

It is helpful to clear out the bin at the end of each class and put its contents in a designated class folder. This keeps the pile of work from overflowing the bin within a few classes, creating a mess and causing panic at the amount of work to be done! Once students receive their graded work, they will either revise it and hand in the batch again, or staple and file the entire assignment in their finished folder.

After you have graded the papers, you can put each one in the writer's working folder before class. If you prefer to return each paper personally, or if your students won't have

Writing Workshop in Middle School © 2013 by Marilyn Pryle • Scholastic

in-class working folders (because they take them home), you can hand out graded papers at the beginning of class or as you circulate around the room. After the day's mini-lesson, you can even use the graded papers as a guide for individual conferencing: as you return each paper, sit with the writer to discuss the revisions. If the paper is finished and needs only to be filed, returning the paper in person gives you a chance to compliment the student on work well done. (An in-depth discussion of individual conferencing appears in Chapter 8.)

Organizing Idea

Have students paper clip their assignments together until it is completely finished. Then they can staple the material together and file it.

Though my color-coding, bin-stacking, clipped-not-stapled methods may seem overly organized, I find them necessary when dealing with large numbers of students. The more structure I can provide outside of class and within the room itself, the more in-class time I will have to spend conferencing with students about their writing.

Plan It!

Where can you designate a handing-in space? On your desk, a nearby windowsill or a shelf?

What kind of container will you use for collecting students' work?

How will you keep the in-flow and out-flow of writing organized? Colored folders? Stacked bins?

Add It!

Return to your room blueprint and add a "handing-in space."

Conferencing Space

Think about where you can conference with students about their work. One method is to circulate and sit with individual students at their desks or computers. In addition, you might want to keep an extra chair by your desk so you can confer with one student without disturbing the others. Also, you may want to make yourself available at your desk for a few minutes each class, so students can approach you when they are ready. Sometimes, when you appear at a student's desk to talk about his or her writing, the student will have no questions at that time. During the course of the class, however, a question may arise. Sometimes students prefer to discuss a certain writing issue with you privately, rather than in close proximity to their neighbors. I've seen these scenarios occur often enough that I make a point of being available at my desk for just a couple minutes each class. If you are sharing a room and cannot move a chair or desk close to your desk, think about an alternative: is there a relatively private spot in the room where you can go if needed? Is there an empty desk, or even just two chairs? Make the best out of whatever is available to create a peaceful space where you can talk to your students about their writing.

Plan It!

Can you plan a space to conference with students in addition to conferencing with them at their desks? Where would it be—by your desk or somewhere else?

Teaching Posters

Add It!
Designate a conferencing space on your room blueprint.

I realized early on in my teacher career that much of my time during individual writing conferences was spent repeating information that I had already formally taught in mini-lessons and that students could understand on their own. My response was to make posters that deal with the most common topics. This isn't too difficult—I use fat markers and write on posterboard. Then I have them laminated. I like to make these posters myself for several reasons. First, I can rarely find a premade poster with the exact information I want on it; if I create it, I can write exactly what I want students to practice. In addition, the writing on store-bought posters is often too small; I can write the information so it is visible from any spot in the room. Finally, manufactured posters are often cluttered with cute but distracting images, which necessitate the small print. By making my own posters, I have complete control over their content and size.

Writing Workshop in Middle School © 2013 by Marilyn Pryle • Scholastic

Below are descriptions of what I've found to be the most useful teaching posters for middle school students. I don't put up every single poster on the first day of class; I usually display only two or three to start, and I put the rest up throughout the year as their content is spotlighted in mini-lessons.

Banned Words Poster

This is the first poster I put up. It has the words *good, bad, things, stuff, cool,* and *great* sitting in the middle of a red circle with a slash through it.

Possessives and Their Homophones Poster

This poster gives examples of the difference between certain possessives and their homophones (*whose/who's, its/it's, their/they're/there,* and *your/you're*). When students ask why I circled *there* on their paper, I promptly send them to this poster to read the examples.

A Lot *Is Two Words Poster*

This small poster reminds students that *a lot,* just like *a little,* is two words!

Transition Words Poster

Early in the year I put up a poster listing the most popular transition words, arranged by category (addition, chronology, contrast, result, conclusion, and so on). For emphasis, I make each category a different color. As a result, when conferring with a student about a piece of writing, I can point out the need for a transition word without have to look up or write out several of these words. I simply ask what *kind* of transition word would best fit and send the student to the poster to browse for words in that category and choose one. While the student does this, I can visit with someone else and check back a bit later.

Commonly Confused Homophones Posters

After a few writing assignments, I hang a poster that lists even more commonly confused homophones than the Possessives and Their Homophones poster, which students can refer to when they have homophone trouble.

Dependent Clauses Poster

This poster shows that dependent clauses beginning with the words *while, when, if, although,* and *even though*

> **Tip**
>
> Make posters on any topics your students struggle with; use the walls as a resource. It is gratifying to see students get up on their own to consult a poster during class.

need an independent clause to stand as complete sentences. I've found that flagging the most commonly used subordinate conjunctions helps students double-check for fragments.

Run-on Sentences Poster

A poster on run-on sentences serves to remind students of how to keep their sentences in check through the proper use of commas, periods, and semicolons.

Posters for Specific Assignments

When we move on to the Character Sketch assignment, I hang a poster called "How to Punctuate Dialogue." Later, when students try an autobiographical account, I put up a poster called "Words Instead of *Said*." As a class, we generate this list of replacement verbs each year; we also create a list for "Words Instead of *Walk*," which I turn into a poster.

Inspirational Décor

If you have space, especially around computers, see if you can find pictures of famous writers or some quotes about writing. In my room, I put small photographs of writers and their major works above each computer, along with an inspirational quote from them. I use author photos from a postcard book I found in a bookstore, but many pictures are available on the Internet. Like most writers, students have moments of drifting off, looking up, or simply staring at a wall. I hope that in these moments some literary thoughts will penetrate their minds, even if it's just the name of an author posted above a computer.

Here are some of my favorite inspirational quotes by writers:

- "If there's a book you really want to read but it hasn't been written yet, then you must write it." —*Toni Morrison*
- "Many times I feel empty, without ideas—and then suddenly the first sentence appears." —*Octavio Paz*
- "Try to be one of the people on whom nothing is lost." —*Henry James*
- "The author must keep his mouth shut when his work starts to speak." —*Friedrich Nietzsche*

I have found quotes in Nancy Atwell's *In the Middle* and Donald Murray's *Shoptalk*, but there are countless sources in books and on the Internet for finding inspirational material. It is best to choose quotes that are inspirational not just for your students but for you as a teacher as well.

How to Start Small

Inspirational décor can be skipped or minimized for now—if you want, choose just one writerly quote, print three copies of it, and post it around your room.

Brainstorm It!

What kinds of posters might help your students? Can you make these or buy something similar, or do you already have something you can use?

Poster	Would Help	I Can Make or Get One
Banned Words	_____	_____
Possessives/Homophones	_____	_____
A Lot is Two Words	_____	_____
Transition Words	_____	_____
Commonly Confused Homophones	_____	_____
Two-Part Sentences	_____	_____
Run-On Sentences	_____	_____
How to Punctuate Dialogue	_____	_____
Words Instead of *Said*	_____	(create with student input)
Words Instead of *Walk*	_____	(create with student input)
Other:	_____	_____

How to Start Small

Out of the list above, choose one poster that would definitely make a difference in your classroom. Circle it, and see if you can make it or buy it. As the year goes on, you can add more, and new ideas for posters will come to you. It might even take two or three years to have all the posters you want. That's OK!

Notebook Bookcase

As I mentioned earlier, each student gets a special notebook just for writing workshop. Ideally, students keep these in a designated bookcase in the classroom (if you don't have one or are sharing a room, a crate can be used). When students enter the room they retrieve the notebooks, and when they leave they replace the notebooks in the bookcase. For efficiency, keep the bookcase ordered by class section.

COMPLETE MATERIALS CHECKLIST

- [ ] A file crate or other container to hold:
    - [ ] Assignment Sheets
    - [ ] Sample Reading/Questions
    - [ ] Prewriting Sheets
- [ ] An easily accessible place for:
    - [ ] Loose-leaf paper
    - [ ] Editing/Revising Checklists
    - [ ] Spelling Practice Sheets
    - [ ] Pens, pencils, highlighters (different colors)
    - [ ] Dictionaries and thesauri
    - [ ] Grammar handbooks
    - [ ] Scissors and tape
- [ ] Wall space or file for working folders
- [ ] Working folders (manila)
- [ ] Computer stations/computer sign-up sheet or schedule
- [ ] Handing-in space
    - [ ] Bin
    - [ ] "Handing-in Order" sign
    - [ ] Paper clips
- [ ] Filing cabinet or other space for finished folders
- [ ] Finished folders
    - [ ] Manila folders
    - [ ] Assignment Log
    - [ ] Stapler
- [ ] Space for conferencing (extra chair at your desk, for example)
- [ ] Space for student notebooks
- [ ] Teaching posters and signs
    - [ ] Banned Words
    - [ ] Possessives/Homophones
    - [ ] *A Lot* is Two Words
    - [ ] Transition Words
    - [ ] Commonly Confused Homophones
    - [ ] Other _____
    - [ ] Dependent Clauses
    - [ ] Run-On Sentences
    - [ ] How to Punctuate Dialogue
    - [ ] Words Instead of *Said**
    - [ ] Words Instead of *Walk**
    - [ ] Other _____
- [ ] Inspirational décor

These posters can be created when the mini-lessons on these topics are taught.

How to Start Small

- Students can take notes in their regular English notebooks instead of buying new ones. Have them set aside a section for writing.

- All the materials listed in this chapter (outside of the actual assignment and its accoutrements) can be gathered and made accessible to your students as the year progresses and needs arise.

- Focus only on the Assignment Headquarters area, making sure to keep a space for the following:

  * Assignment Sheets

  * Prewriting Sheets

  * Sample Reading/Questions

  * Editing/Revising Checklists

  * Loose-leaf paper

  You could even hand these out as a complete packet if you want students to begin and end together, and you wouldn't even need a designated Assignment Headquarters area.

- Focus just on your first two assignments for now.

Chapter 6

Launching the Workshop: The First Three Days, and Beyond

I spend the first few days of class explaining the workshop routine, preparing students mentally for the work ahead, and enthusiastically stressing the importance and joy of writing. This chapter details how I structure the first few days of my workshop—and hopefully these ideas will help you structure yours.

The First Day: Passion for the Writing Life

On Day 1, I express my conviction for the writing workshop. I believe this goes a long way in setting expectations about a work ethic and expected classroom behavior. My passion and reverence for the written word—any word, especially theirs, written with sincerity and effort—sets the tone for the year.

Here are the objectives for Day 1:

- Communicate the importance of the writing workshop
- Give an overview of the workshop process
- Conduct a scavenger hunt
- Set up finished folders and assignment logs, assign computers
- Read a poem
- Distribute writing surveys

Communicate the Importance of the Writing Workshop

After settling the students in their seats, I give them the Welcome to Writing Workshop sheet shown on the next page and focus on the first two paragraphs.

Writing Workshop in Middle School © 2013 by Marilyn Pryle • Scholastic

Welcome to Writing Workshop!

Welcome! You are very fortunate to have time in school just for writing—it is a wonderful way to learn more about yourself and the world we live in. Not only will you improve in writing skills this year, you will also improve in *everything*, because writing is about thinking. When you become a better writer, you become a better thinker. And when you are a better thinker, your whole life is better!

This year, you will be writing many pieces about the topics you know well—yourself, your family, your friends, your hobbies, your talents, and your experiences! YOU are the expert in this class. We will read work from many writers who came before you, and we will experiment with many forms and styles of writing. I'll be there to help you every step of the way.

Here are some facts about the class:

- You will need a single-subject notebook without spirals. You will leave your notebook in the classroom—you don't even have to carry it back and forth!

- You will complete writing assignments that I give you—but YOU will choose each topic. This means you can write about the people, places, ideas, things, and experiences in your own life.

- You will work at your own pace in class. When you are finished with one assignment, you will move to the next one on your own.

- You will do most, or all, of your writing in the class. Think of this writing workshop as a woodworking class—all the tools are in this classroom, and you come here and use them to create.

- You will not have regular homework! The only work that you'll do outside of class is at the end of the quarter, if there are any assignments that you did not get finished in class. Even though you will each work at your own pace, you will all have the same number of assignments to finish each quarter.

- I will grade your work and give it back to you. You will then have a chance to revise it for points back. You must achieve a minimum of 90 on every assignment. It is possible to get a 100 on every assignment!

- Each writing assignment is broken down into small steps. We'll take one at a time, and I will help you at every step.

You will learn a lot about yourself this year, and about writing as well. I am really looking forward to helping you and reading about your ideas and lives. Have fun and work hard!

Setting the Tone

Ms. P.: I want you to realize how special it is to have an extra class (*or use the phrase "extra class time" here if applicable*) just for writing. Many schools don't have anything like this. Your success in writing workshop does not depend on whether you're a "good" writer or not. (*I use air quotes for emphasis.*) How "good" you think you are as a writer does not matter at all. What we will do this year, all of us, is improve, and go deeper into our writing. And do you know what happens then? When you become a better *writer*, you become a better *thinker*. Think about that: when you become a better *writer*, you become a better *thinker*. Writing is thinking. A lot of times we don't even know what we think about something until we write it down. And what happens when you become a better thinker? Well, you become better at *everything*: you become a better friend, a better son, a better daughter, a better sister, a better brother, a better boyfriend, a better girlfriend, a better athlete, a better mathematician—do you see? When your mind is better, *everything* is better. That's what we're going to do in this class.

As writing teachers, we must feel a passion for the written word, whether we consider ourselves "writers" or not. Certainly, we are all writers: on any given day, we communicate several times through the written (or typed) word. We communicate not only practical information but also feelings, inferences, opinions, questions, and predictions. We figure problems out as we write, we plan the future, we get just the right thought down in an e-mail or journal entry, and we feel a sense of satisfaction. Whether we realize it or not, we grow.

Think About It: Your Own Writing

When do you write during any given day? What do you write about? List as many ideas as possible, including journals, e-mail, marginalia, sticky notes, grocery lists, to-do lists, texts, poems, stories, lesson plans, reports, research papers, agendas, thank-you notes, sick notes, reflection papers, online reviews, homework, greeting cards, and so on.

Now think about the benefit all of this writing brings to your life—not just for remembering information but also for living, for learning, for interacting with others. Writing a college or graduate paper, as stressful as it sometimes is, helps us internalize the information and ultimately grow as professionals and people. We've all experienced this. Writing our feelings out on a greeting card to a person we love elevates our own spirits. Writing a cohesive review of a product we enjoyed (or hated!) gives satisfaction and a feeling of having contributed something to the world at large. Writing not only affects the reader; the act of writing also affects the writer. We already know this to be true, but our students may not.

What's more, writing workshop might be the only time in our students' day when they slow down and think in silence. It takes time to write, and a quiet mind. These are lost luxuries. And good writing often requires *waiting*, a skill that is frequently neglected in our culture. To slow down, to reflect, to look closely at the world—writing workshop might be your students' only time to do these things. This is an absolute gift, and as teachers, we must communicate our conviction in the benefits of a "writing life," not only through our words but also through our patience, encouragement, and belief in the ability of each student to write meaningfully.

One thing that has helped me stay connected with the act of writing and my students' journeys is to do the writing assignments myself at home as students do them. Writing out my own character sketch, autobiographical essay, process essay, and letter for social action feels gratifying. Plus, I can use my prewriting, and even my rough drafts, as models for students—it is so important for them to see their teacher trying and erring, revising, and sharing parts of her own life. It not only keeps me enthusiastic about the assignments themselves, it also builds community in the classroom. As teachers, we are already overloaded with work, but I don't think of writing as part of my schoolwork. Even if you can only try one assignment a quarter, I think you will feel the benefits of it.

Teaching Tip

Try to actually write your own pieces along with your students! This will connect you not only with the lessons but also with your students.

Give an Overview of the Workshop Process

I read through the Welcome to Writing Workshop sheet and give students an overview of the class—that they will complete a certain number of assignments and that they can work at their own pace, though all work must be completed by the end of the quarter. I explain that some students will have to take work home at some point, or come in after class to do the work. They are responsible for figuring out how to get the work done. It also means that they should not waste one moment of class time; they must work hard every class in order to avoid an avalanche of work toward the end.

I also tell students that they will be expected to revise their work, and that revision and the process they use is part of the grade. I emphasize my belief that the mind needs time to work, that the mind works subconsciously after we stop writing. When we sit down to write the next day, very often the answer that was previously so elusive appears, seemingly by magic. Here's how I explain the magic of revision to students:

How Inspiration (or Revision) Works

Ms. P.: Let's say, for example, you're writing about your grandmother cooking her favorite recipe for potato dumplings, and you can remember how her hair was pinned back and that her shoes were brown with old laces, and that her glasses were dirty and her eyes were green and happy, but for the life of you, you cannot remember the color of her favorite apron, ruffled around the edges and permanently tied at the top, so all she would have to do was slip it over her head and tie the bottom. You spend several minutes trying to see it but you just can't, and you think maybe you'll just make up a color, like blue, blue with large green leaves. Then you forget about the whole thing; you go about your normal life until the next day, when you spread out your papers and wonder where you left off, and bam! There it is, in your mind, the apron— yellow, yellow with small white flowers. You scramble through your draft and write it in. This is how the mind works—when we're not thinking about something specific, when we're at basketball or dinner or online—it's trying to remember the color. The mind does this not just with details but also for sentences and verbs and introductions and characters and clinchers. This is why we come back to our writing and try to revise.

Then I give students the Writing Workshop: How It Works sheet shown on the next page. Display copies of this sheet are posted around the room for the entire year, so I can remind students of what they should be doing if they have drifted off track. After the first few weeks, most students have internalized the routine. Until then, this page is invaluable, and students will consult it frequently.

I read through the steps, trying not to bombard students with information but still giving them the gist of the class. All the small details will become clear as time passes.

Timesaving Tip!

Use the two handouts on pages 77 and 81 as your handouts for Parents' Night.

Conduct a Scavenger Hunt

A scavenger hunt is a great way for students to explore the room for themselves while being directed to important resources. (A sample Writing Workshop Scavenger Hunt sheet appears on page 82.) Students can locate their working folders, the assignment crate, their finished folders, various teaching posters and quotations, and so on. If you are traveling and don't have many writing workshop materials in the room, you may want to forgo the scavenger hunt and point out these main necessities.

Writing Workshop in Middle School © 2013 by Marilyn Pryle • Scholastic

Writing Workshop: How It Works

Each time you come in to class, here's what you will do:

1. Get your notebook from the bookshelf and any papers you filed in your **working folder**.

2. Take notes during the mini-lesson.

3. Continue working on your assignment.

4. When you finish an assignment, paper clip all the papers for it and take them to the handing-in space.

5. When you are ready to start a new assignment, go to the assignment crate and get the material for the next assignment (all assignments are numbered; go in order).

6. When I return a paper, and you need to revise it for points back, do your revisions, print it again, and hand in the entire group of papers again.

7. When I return a finished paper to you with a final grade (90 or above), staple everything together, and place it in your **finished folder**. Record it on the assignment log and put it in your file. Return the file to its proper alphabetic place.

8. Go back to #3 if you're still working on another assignment, or #5 if you're ready for a new one.

Name _____ Date _____

Writing Workshop Scavenger Hunt

Find the following and identify its location:

1. Your working folder

2. The assignment crate

3. The printer

4. Highlighters

5. A thesaurus

6. Your finished folder

7. Loose-leaf paper

8. The notebook bookcase

9. Editing/Revising Checklists

10. Spelling Practice Sheets

Answer these questions and tell where you found the answer:

11. Which is the correct spelling: *a lot* or *alot*?

12. What is the meaning of *its*?

13. When you hand in an assignment, what should go on top of the pile?

14. What's a homophone for *peace*?

15. What kind of a transition word is *although*?

16. What are the dates of Mark Twain's birth and death?

17. At what age did the author Willa Cather think that you have all the material you need to write?

18. Think of your own question and write it below. Tell where the answer can be found.

Set up Finished Folders and Assignment Logs, Assign Computers

After the scavenger hunt, I distribute the manila folders, which will be their finished folders. Students neatly print their names on the tabs while I hand out and briefly describe the assignment logs. The kids then write their names and the year at the top of the assignment logs and staple them to the inside covers of the finished folders. Finally, I assign a computer to each student. If your students have limited computer access, explain your plan for how they will type their assignments.

> **Tip**
> Round up several staplers from other teachers so that setting up the finished folders goes smoothly.

Read a Poem

If there is time, I like to end the first class with a poem or two, such as Walt Whitman's "When I Heard the Learn'd Astronomer" or Mary Oliver's "The Summer Day." Both of these poems reinforce the tone of the class—Whitman's by reinforcing the idea of trust in the self and one's own perception, and Oliver's by emphasizing each person's "one precious life." Both poems also employ essential techniques of poetry, such as alliteration, repetition, and the use of sensory details, all of which are interesting to explore if time permits.

Using a poem to end the class brings the first day full circle to the beginning, when I emphasized the power of writing. Choose poems that you know and love—or, if you wish, choose a short bit of memoir or fiction.

Distribute Writing Surveys

If you have a larger block of time for writing workshop, you may be able to do a writing survey in class; otherwise, you can assign it for homework. A sample writing survey appears in the Appendix on page 159. The aim of the survey is to help students 1) begin to recognize themselves as writers if they do not already do so, and 2) analyze their writing perceptions and behaviors. Emphasize to students that there are no wrong answers; they should honestly record their feelings, beliefs, and experiences. The purpose of the survey is to get students thinking about themselves and their habits rather than for you to evaluate them. In completing the survey, students will start to become aware of their own routines for writing: Do they plan? Do they revise? Do they save everything for the last minute? Additionally, the survey demonstrates to students that they write throughout the day, for myriad reasons. I like to keep these surveys until the end of the year, after students are familiar with the workshop process and confident in their abilities to use tools to write organized, meaningful pieces. It is interesting to watch them read their initial thoughts about their writing selves.

Then, to conclude the year, I give an end-of-the-year survey so students can reflect on their overall progress and attitudes towards writing. A sample of this survey is on page 160.

The Second Day

The goal of the second day is help students see that the stuff of their lives is plentiful and interesting, and the perfect raw material for writing.

Here are the objectives for Day 2:

- Discussion: Where does writing come from?
- Topics for Writing list

Discussion: Where Does Writing Come From?

On the second day, we talk about the source of writing. You can discuss this with the class, or have students freewrite and discuss in small groups, depending on your available time. There are some wonderful short reflections on this question, notably "Where Does Writing Hide?" from Georgia Heard's *Writing Toward Home*. Many students will suggest answers such as, "It comes from your imagination," which of course is true, but what you want to ultimately suggest to them is that writing mostly comes from our own lives—the sights, sounds, smells, people, memories, and feelings we all have swirling around in our minds and hearts. What's more, the ordinary details of our lives are just as important as the extraordinary; to write something meaningful, one does not have to have lived an unusual life, but one must learn to look closely at the life one does have. The implication of this is that *each of us has something to write about.* We do not need to have lived through something extraordinary to qualify as writers; we need only to learn how to see the ordinary with fresh eyes. Some students may not believe this at first, but you must reiterate it all year: *Each of us has something to say. The stuff of your life is important enough to write about.*

Keep an eye on your discussion time here—if you have a fifty-minute class, you should only spend about ten minutes discussing the idea of writing from one's own life. The second part of the class, which involves actually listing the "stuff" of one's life, is vital and will take about thirty-five minutes or so.

> Let your mantra for the year be:
> *You have something to write.*
> *Your own life is interesting enough*
> *to write about, if you look*
> *closely at it.*

Topics for Writing List

Ideally everyone has brought a notebook; if not, provide paper, which students can transfer into their notebooks. Now that students are convinced of (or at least exposed to!) the idea that writers use the details of their own lives in their writing, they create a Topics for Writing list. This extended inventory of possible writing topics for each student will serve them the entire year. Students catalog the people, places, experiences, things, opinions, feelings, and memories in their lives. I first learned about this technique from Nancie Atwell's *In the Middle*; Atwell recommends giving students silent time to write whatever comes to mind.

Writing Workshop in Middle School © 2013 by Marilyn Pryle • Scholastic

I've found that guiding students through this process by asking a series of detailed questions helps them write as much as possible (see page 86 for my "Topics for Writing" questions).

For any assignment, students can consult this inventory for ideas. If, during a conference, students declare that they "have nothing to write," you can direct them to their Topics for Writing list. Of course, students can go off the list for ideas as well; they need not confine themselves to it, but it usually acts as a fertile starting point.

I love to do this exercise at the beginning of the year because it is nonthreatening and even easy—at this point, writing an essay or poem might seem unachievable to some kids, but writing a list about what they already know seems feasible. Plus, students are still in the state of excited possibility and are willing to go along.

To help students brainstorm their Topic for Writing lists, follow these steps:

Step 1: Students set up a table of contents page in their notebooks.

First, have students create a table of contents on the first page in their notebooks. Instruct them to leave two full pages (four sides, front and back) for the table of contents and to begin their first entry on the third full page. On that page, have students write "Topics for Writing" at the top and the page number 1 in the top right corner. Then have them flip back to the contents page and record that title and page number. This practice continues all year: whenever you teach a mini-lesson, have students take notes for the mini-lesson on a new page in their notebooks, number that page, and record the mini-lesson title and page number in their table of contents.

Step 2: Guide students in creating a Topics for Writing list.

Next, have students turn back to their Topics for Writing page. To help them create this list, I usually say something like this:

Ms. P.: Our first job is to create a Topics for Writing list. This is going to be a giant list of things from your life. Try to relax—take a deep breath and let it out—and write whatever pops into your mind as I ask you some questions. Really, you can just write anything. There are no right or wrong answers here. And all you have to do is write a word or two on each line, or maybe a phrase—you don't have to write sentences or paragraphs—just a list of words. You are the only ones who are going to read this list, so you are the only ones who have to understand what the words mean.

OK—let's start here: What in your life do you think might be interesting to write about? See if you can think of a few things, and write one on each line—a word or phrase.

Students should be writing or thinking quietly during this process. All year, I emphasize to students that when it is time to write, they must be silent and let one another write. They cannot come up with their own words when someone else is talking to them, or when they are talking to someone else. I enforce this from the beginning. With most classes, after the first few weeks, students accept silence as another part of the routine.

I begin with the broad question, "What in your life do you think might be interesting to write about?" because for some students it covers all the big, important, obvious answers (which might become well-written pieces nonetheless). Once they've written down these major events, though, students can start to dig deeper for the buried gems. Some students may not know what to write and will sit uncomfortably. Either way, after a few minutes, begin to pose the rest of the questions shown below, speaking slowly, giving students time to write. (You do not need to have students number the list; I have numbered the questions only for ease of reference.) Wait until all students seem to have finished answering a question before moving on to the next one.

Questions to Help Generate Topics for Writing

Read slowly and give students time to write!

1. Who are some important people in your life? Name them. Family, friends? How about pets? (Individuals can be living or deceased.)

2. Who are some interesting people in your life? They could be people you are close to, or people who are acquaintances, such as the guy who lives across the street who sings a song called "Mr. Pancake" to the tune of "Mr. Sandman" to call his dog home. What makes them interesting?

3. What are some of your favorite places? Name them. Think of indoors; think of outdoors. Add a few details if they come to mind. What are some interesting places you've seen, even if you didn't like them? What are some places you hate?

4. What are some of your favorite belongings, things that mean a lot to you? Some jewelry? A necklace, watch, bracelet, ring? Something in your room? A piece of clothing?

5. What are some of your favorite movies? What are some movies you didn't like? Do you have a favorite play?

6. What are some of your favorite books? Favorite short stories? (It may help to name some from previous years' curriculums.) Favorite poems?

7. Who is your favorite band or singer? Whom do you dislike?

8. What in the school would you change if you could? What do you wish your school had?

9. What would you change in your town? What do you wish your town had? What do you wish your town *didn't* have?

10. What in our country would you change? Any laws or policies? Should any laws be added?

11. What makes you angry or annoyed?

Writing Workshop in Middle School © 2013 by Marilyn Pryle • Scholastic

12. What are your hobbies? What are things you know how to do well?

13. What else are you good at? What else do you know about, even if you think it's no big deal—such as delivering papers, or babysitting, or playing card games?

14. At home, what do you know a lot about?

15. In school, what are your favorite subjects? Which subjects are easiest for you?

16. Can you remember any dreams you've had that stand out in your mind? What happened?

17. Do you ever daydream? In the car, in school, or somewhere else? What do you think about?

18. Try to remember a time in your life that was sad. Write a phrase or two. If you have more than one example, write both.

19. Try to remember a time that was scary. Write a phrase or two.

20. Try to remember a time that was difficult, or a time when you had to meet a big challenge.

21. Note a time in your life that was funny—it could involve your family or friends. Maybe you have a few examples. Jot down a phrase for each.

22. Think of a time that was really joyful or happy. Maybe you can think of two or three times. What were they? What happened? Write a few phrases.

23. Now think of a time that felt peaceful—when you felt totally settled, calm, and at peace. You weren't worried about anything; you felt all was right with the world. When was it? Who was there? Write a few words or phrases.

Teaching Idea

Write your own Topics for Writing and share it with the students as they create theirs.

Prior to class, type your own responses to each question to share with students. When I do this, I take note of when most pens have stopped moving for a given question, then I show my own answer on the projector. I reveal my answers question-by-question to keep students focused on the moment. I have found this practice to be valuable for three reasons. First, very often one of my answers will spark an idea in a student's mind; I see several students adding to their own lists the moment I read mine. Second, it shows students that I am willing to show them the stuff of my life: my thoughts, memories, hobbies, and so on. (Of course, my list is deliberately age-appropriate and not awkwardly over-revealing.) I have taken the first step in trusting them, and I hope they will trust me with their stories and thoughts. Third, it communicates my belief in our group as a community of writers. They are writers; I am a writer; this is what writers do. They can see that I practice what I preach. At the end of the session, I show students the notebook I keep for running ideas. A sampling of my list appears on the next page; of course, it evolves, but you get the idea!

Ms. Pryle's Topics for Writing

1.	Tim		*Les Misérables*
	Gavin	**6.**	*Cry, the Beloved Country* by Alan Paton
	Tiernan	**7.**	The Rolling Stones
	Mom, Dad	**8.**	bring back Latin
	Nanny, Poppa	**9.**	an inexpensive swimming club
	Gram, Gramps	**10.**	National driving w/o cell phones law
2.	Matt, John, Tom	**11.**	annoying: ungrateful people
	Mary	**12.**	writing poems
	Mr. Stevens (teacher)	**13.**	playing Boggle
	the woman at the coffee shop	**14.**	organizing
	Mr. Price (neighbor)	**15.**	English, math
	John (custodian)	**16.**	dream of swimming in air
3.	my backyard: pine trees, apple tree	**17.**	becoming a marathon runner
	Impressionist Room in MFA in Boston	**18.**	Sitting with Alice when she couldn't
	woods/pond at my parent's house		remember us
	Kathmandu—rooftops, mountains, dirt roads	**19.**	When Matt was sick
	Rodin Museum in Philadelphia	**20.**	Time trials at Scranton
	Steamtown Yoga room	**21.**	Zebra costume with Patti
	breakfast room—bright, open	**22.**	When Virginia called about the paper
	our old house when I was 5—grapevines		The four of us at Scranton Yankees
4.	Nanny's ring	**23.**	Virginia Beach at dawn
5.	*The Shawshank Redemption*		Holding Gavin for the first time

By the end of this session, most students will have a list at least a page long; some will have a full two or even three pages. I usually then give the following advice:

Ms. P.: During the year, if new ideas come into your mind, you should add them to your list. This is what happens with writers—you get a new idea in the middle of writing something else, or in the middle of the day. Since you are writers, this will happen to you, too. When it does, jot down the idea somewhere, somehow, and when there is time, add it to your Topics for Writing list.

Jim: I don't think I'm going to be thinking of anything school-related when I'm out of school.

Ms. P.: Wait and see! I promise it will happen, and if you pay attention to it, it will happen more and more. It's like a muscle: the more you use it, the more it works. I call this an "idea muscle." It never fails if you try.

Jim: Where do I write it? Am I supposed to write stuff on my hand?

Ms. P.: Wherever you can—I carry a little notebook around with me. (*I show them the notebook I keep in my purse.*) You could look for the nearest paper and pen, or grab a receipt, napkin, movie ticket—anything. And you only need to write a word or two to help you remember. This is what creative people do. And all of you are creative.

Jim: I'm not!

Ms. P.: How many of you have ever gotten an idea for something while you were in the middle of something else—for example, you get an idea for a new song, or a new picture to draw, or a new way to arrange your room, or something new you want to try in a sport? (*Some hands raise.*) That's your idea muscle working! Our minds are always trying to give us new ideas. We just have to pay attention to them.

Jim: I don't know. I don't think my mind is like that.

Ms. P.: I'd like all of you to try an experiment. Ask your mind for new ideas, and for a whole day write down anything that pops up. Don't ask yourself if it's a good idea or not; just write it. Then ask again on a second day, and again on a third, and keep writing everything. Give it three days of really trying, and see what happens. (*This won't fail if students really try, and it usually sparks an interesting discussion a few days later.*)

Ms. P.: Now, take a look at your Topics for Writing list. Most of you have a couple of pages or more. You should feel proud of this! These are just some of the things you know a lot about. And in most of the areas on your list, you know more than I do! You are the experts here. You know enough right now to be a writer. Never doubt that. Don't ever say you don't have anything to write. You have your whole life.

> **Tip**
>
> When you start the next mini-lesson, be sure to remind students to leave an extra page blank for their expanding Topics for Writing list.

The value of this list throughout the year is immense. For any assignment or genre (nonfiction, fiction, poetry), students can consult this list for ideas. Sometimes it is difficult to summon a topic on the spot, with the parameters and time limit of a specific assignment weighing on the writer. For example, when students come to the Autobiographical Account assignment, they sometimes don't know which moment out of their entire lives to choose to write about. However, as they skim their Topics for Writing list, they might notice something to turn into an interesting story, especially toward the end where they have brainstormed times that were scary, funny, difficult, or joyful. Likewise, in the face of the Letter for Social Action assignment, students may feel intimidated about actually writing a letter to an authority figure, but by consulting their thoughts from the Topics for Writing list, they may become more motivated after reading what they wrote about their school, town, or country. Students write the Topics for Writing list freely and calmly, without the pressure of having to "write" anything, and it serves as a reliable resource and a touchstone throughout the year.

The Third Day: Begin the First Assignment

The first assignment I give my students is usually the introductory letter. I begin by reading them the sample reading, a letter I have written to them, introducing myself. (After this, students read the sample reading on their own.) For a mini-lesson, I share the brainstorming and grouping I did for this letter, and we trace ideas from the brainstorming to the final copy. Students then try brainstorming on their own, and the workshop begins. For the next several classes, I will provide students with explicit directions and answer questions about the workshop routine so the process firmly takes root.

A few weeks into the year, when the workshop is running smoothly, the detailed work of these early days comes to fruition. Students move around the classroom comfortably and with focus, often surprising visitors to the classroom that adolescents can work so productively and earnestly on their own. This situation is achievable because in the beginning, I consistently reinforce all procedures and boundaries. During the first two or three assignments, I monitor students at every step. I repeat the routine constantly, directing students to the Writing Workshop: How It Works sheet; I subtract points for any task students skip (they can usually earn these back); and I do not tolerate disruptions.

Beyond: The Workshop in Motion

Eventually, when the workshop is in full swing, it will look like the description on page 10.

Preparing for the first days of class can be overwhelming, so here is a list of what you will need to get started:

CHECKLIST OF MATERIALS FOR THE FIRST THREE DAYS

DAY 1	DAY 2	DAY 3
☐ Welcome to Writing Workshop sheet	☐ (Optional) *Where Does Writing Hide?* by Georgia Heard	The first writing assignment:
☐ Finished folders	☐ Extra paper for students without notebooks	☐ Assignment sheet
☐ Assignment logs for inside the folder	☐ Questions for Topics for Writing list	☐ Sample reading/questions
☐ Extra staplers	☐ Your own Topics for Writing list to show students	☐ Prewriting sheets (if needed)
☐ Computer assignments/ sign-up sheets		☐ Mini-lesson prepared
☐ Writing Workshop: How It Works sheet		
☐ Photocopies of poems (or some other writing)		
☐ Writing Survey		

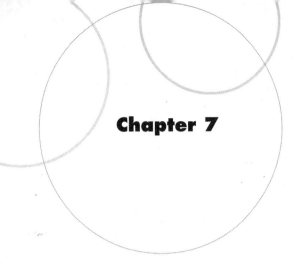

Chapter 7

Using Rubrics and Grading to Help Students Revise

Grading writing can be a delicate matter. To put a number on a person's effort and the product of his or her self-expression seems harsh. To quantify the internal growth that takes place as an adolescent finds a sense of voice and learns how to use it seems absurd. And yet, we must. Few of us have the time or space to house voluminous portfolios for over a hundred students; moreover, the powers that be demand that we produce a score that can be averaged with other scores in order for parents and society to evaluate students' progress and standing. It is the way of the world.

I asked myself how I could preserve the sense of safety and trust needed for the creative process if students in any way feared what grade they would get in the end. How could they write if there was a possibility of getting it wrong, of making mistakes that would be costly? I decided the answer must be an assurance that all points are obtainable for everyone. Yes, the points must be earned, but anyone can earn them with effort. And if students don't earn them at first, they can do what it takes to earn them later. I decided to shift the focus from the one-shot attempt at a perfect finished product to an ongoing effort within the process of writing.

> In the end, it is effort, not talent, that will determine a student's final grade.

Goals of Grading

To do this, I determined the following three goals:

1. **The grade should reflect what has been taught both in the current assignment and past assignments.** The rubric should reflect every aspect of the assignment sheet and every applicable technique students have learned to that

Writing Workshop in Middle School © 2013 by Marilyn Pryle • Scholastic

point. There should be no surprises, no tricks to figure out; students should receive points for practicing exactly what they are learning.

2. **Points are rewarded for effort during the process of writing.** Students get points based on effort, for following the path of the writing process charted by each assignment sheet as best they can. (Knowing their individual abilities is our responsibility as teachers.) Thus, to get full points, students have to be working at their own personal edge.

3. **Students are allowed to earn points back with revisions.** Grades must be revisable, just as the writing is revisable. Students should have a chance to push their writing further and be rewarded for it. Revision reinforces the writing process; why not demonstrate that to students through grades?

As mentioned in the last chapter, I tell students (and parents) in the beginning of the year that it is possible for every student to get 100 on every assignment, by trying and retrying, and by working on each step. Skipping steps, working quickly and mindlessly, or being lazy will not be rewarded with points. I also reassure students that there will be no time limit (besides the end of the quarter) for revising. They can revise a paper as many times as they choose. If they work hard, they will not fail.

By using a rubric and having revisable grades, you can push students to give their best effort. For example, suppose the rubric for a Free Verse Poem assignment calls for the poem to include similes. If a student simply slaps the first two similes that come to her mind into the poem in order to satisfy the rubric, you can respond in one of two ways:

> **Student Note**
>
> "It helps to revise for points back so I can fix my own mistakes instead of you doing it for me."
>
> —Kullen H.

- First, you can check the student's prewriting sheet to trace the similes to a specific sensory detail and help her focus on that sensory detail in a more meaningful way. You may find that the student was hasty or careless in completing the work on the prewriting sheet, which often is the case when the end product is weak. You could then send the student back to the prewriting stage of the assignment. The first round of grades you give will reflect the lack of effort in the prewriting.

- If the student's prewriting seems adequate, you could deduct points for using clichés, if that applies to the similes. Then encourage the student to revise the similes and thus get those points back. This would take some additional thinking, but the student would be rewarded for the effort.

Therefore, through grades, you can push students to try more, to think harder.

> Instead of viewing grading as a burden, use grades as a tool to motivate students to do their best work. Students come to realize that in the workshop, more effort always means a better grade.

In order to maintain continuity throughout the year and to establish that sense of writing as a routine that spirals deeper with each attempt, I use the same five categories on the rubric for all genres. Depending on the genre, the categories might have varying applications, but the general meaning of each category remains the same throughout all assignments. The five categories, worth 20 points each, are structure, process, description, spelling, and grammar.

For each assignment, list specific skills from current and past mini-lessons in parentheses after each category on the rubric. This tells students exactly what you're grading them on for a particular assignment. In addition, when grading, you can circle students' weak skills from these lists so they can see precisely where they lost points. Below is an example of the rubric from the Compare-and-Contrast Essay assignment sheet, which I introduced in Chapter 4:

ASSIGNMENT RUBRIC	PRELIMINARY GRADE	REVISED GRADE
Structure (*organization, paragraphs, length, font*) 20 pts.		
Process (*questions, brainstorm/group, draft, Editing/Revising Checklist*) 20 pts.		
Description (*introduction, conclusion, banned/cliché, transition words*) 20 pts.		
Spelling 20 pts.		
Grammar (*punctuation, capitals, sentences*) 20 pts.		
TOTAL		

This rubric tells students that they are responsible for writing cohesive paragraphs, each focused on one idea, which they would have learned in the mini-lessons leading up to this assignment. Whatever you introduce or emphasize in an assignment's mini-lessons should appear in the rubric, along with all other pertinent skills students have learned thus far. Again, the consistency is in the categories: the same five categories are broad enough to accommodate all genres.

Writing Workshop in Middle School © 2013 by Marilyn Pryle • Scholastic

Rubric Categories

Structure

Structure primarily encompasses length and font. For middle school, I usually require a minimum of one typed page for essays, one and a half pages for fiction, and twenty to thirty lines for poems and list length requirements clearly on the rubric. If there is no length requirement, some students will turn in work that is entirely too brief and shallow and gives them barely anything to work with in revision. The longer we write, the better the chance that we will stumble upon a usable idea or mine an example to its most meaningful point. I sometimes set maximum levels as well, as many students will not only surpass the minimum but also continue indefinitely! (In these cases, they sometimes need help narrowing their topics.) The font stipulation relates to length: ten lines of one font could equal an entire page of another; for uniformity, students write in 12-point Times New Roman.

> **Differentiate!**
> Structure can be differentiated by requiring longer work for more advanced students and perhaps only a paragraph for less advanced students or beginning ELLs.

Structure also includes organization and ordering. And depending on the assignment, the meaning of these terms may vary. Organization could refer to paragraphs, stanzas, or plot; it could refer to the progression of examples or reasons in an essay; it could refer to the stray ideas scattered throughout a piece that need to be cleaned up.

Finally, structure also encompasses special formats, like letters.

Process

> **Differentiate!**
> To achieve full points in the Process category, some students will need to do several revisions, while others will revise only a couple times. Revisions will vary for every student on every assignment, depending on his or her strengths.

This is a vital category. It allows me to reward students for following the steps I have laid out for them, which is, of course, what makes the workshop run at all. Process emphasizes writing as progression. I tell students that they should get full points in this category every time they write, since success here depends not on knowledge or talent but on effort and conscientiousness. This category includes the completion of the sample reading and its accompanying questions, prewriting, drafting, revising, and completing an Editing/Revising Checklist.

Description

Description gets right to the heart of any paper. It's the category that fluctuates most with each genre, but it generally denotes a description of content. In an essay, description includes the introduction, conclusion, and details of the body paragraphs. In fiction, it includes character and setting. In poetry, it can include similes, personification, and sensory detail.

From the beginning of the year, avoiding banned words and clichés falls under this category; soon after this comes transition words.

The bigger the skill, the more points I give it: if a paragraph needs one more example, I might subtract five points, but if someone hands in an essay devoid of an introduction, I subtract ten points. Individual student differences play a role, too: if a lower-level student tries some new verbs, even though they aren't the strongest possible choices for the piece, I congratulate her. A more advanced student who uses those same verbs without much thought or effort might lose five points and be sent back to revise them.

> **Differentiate!**
>
> Description provides a wide range of choices. Look back at the compare-and-contrast essays on pages 46 and 47. For instance, you could simplify the rubric on page 44 for students who struggle by focusing on one or two aspects, such as introduction and transition words.

Spelling

Twenty points may seem like a lot to award simply for spelling words correctly, but, alas, it is appropriate. I used to lump spelling and grammar together, only to have spelling dominate the category and make the whole idea of editing seem impossible.

As I explained in the section on Spelling Practice Sheets in the previous chapter, I do not feel it unreasonable to expect papers to be handed in with few or no spelling errors. In most cases, a spelling error reflects apathy: physical apathy in the refusal to get up and get a dictionary, or mental apathy in the refusal to run the spell-checker feature or to pay attention to the spell-checker as it changes words. Sometimes, though, an honest mistake and, in turn, a learnable moment, arises when students encounter an unknown homophone. Usually, however, laziness is the culprit.

This observation does not apply to students with learning disabilities, of course; every student's individual ability becomes a factor on the rubric. For the average or above-average student, I deduct five points for each misspelled word, up to the category's maximum of four misspelled words. Students must correct the words in the next draft and write them each five times on a Spelling Practice Sheet. If students have more than four misspelled words, they must still correct those words and write them out on the Spelling Practice Sheet; but they can't lose any additional points in this category. At the same time, they can't gain the full points for this category until they correct and rewrite all misspelled words. For learning disabled students, however, I adjust my grading criteria. For example, I might grade these students solely on one orthographic pattern, or one section only.

Spelling has its own category because I want students to curb bad habits of inattention, carelessness, and sloppy editing. On many state

> **Differentiate!**
>
> For some students, you may want to only grade for a certain spelling pattern, or grade spelling in the first paragraph only. You can also focus on five words in any given assignment for the student to work with.

standardized tests, students are permitted to use dictionaries; I want them to be adept at this. But it's more important that students use language purposefully and develop the habit of seeking answers for what is unknown to them.

Grammar

This is a large category that refers to mechanics, usage, and conventions—everything but spelling. It is a category that students usually max out on point-wise during the first round of grading. As with all categories, I can tailor grammar to the needs of individual students, the specific assignment, and my own preferences. Some skills are always required, such as punctuation and capitalization. Other skills are learned in the mini-lessons for a particular assignment. I often include a blank line at the end of the list, so I can add a grammar skill that a student needs to work on.

Differentiate!

For students who have command of conventions, use this category to push them to combine short sentences and vary structure. For struggling students, grade for only one or two conventions per assignment, or grade for every convention, but only the first paragraph or two.

Differentiation

By allowing you to put your feelings and judgment about a student's work into numbers, the rubric can give you a sense of empowerment. As the teacher, you have control over the rubric. You can grade each student on as little or as much as you wish—for the bulk of students, this amount will be the same, but for some students, it will be different. For example, for a student who has difficulty spelling due to a learning disability, you can base the spelling grade on the first paragraph only; for another challenged student, you can set the length at half a page. For a student with a perfect score on conventions, you can focus on the rubric's Description category to raise the quality of his or her sensory detail. A rubric allows you to push each student to his or her edge, to act as a coach spurring your athletes along. It is your responsibility to know what that edge is for each student, and by being attentive to your students, you quickly will.

The Benefits of Grading With a Rubric

As a teacher, you will appreciate the efficiency of a rubric, and its fairness. A student who struggles with punctuation, for example, will not receive a failing grade on a paper based on punctuation alone. Since grammar and mechanics are only one-fifth of the total grade, the punctuation-challenged pupil can still get an 80 if all other aspects of the paper are satisfactory. Likewise, a student can never get a 50 solely due to spelling. Of course, the components in any category don't have to *add up* to 20; 20 is simply the number at which you stop subtracting points. However, I've also learned to ensure that students do not use the rubric as a crutch. For example, if a student hands in a carelessly written one-paragraph essay, I subtract full points from the Structure category (for length) and from the Description category (for the lack of ideas). I often remove points from the Process category as well, since students who hand in cursory work often skip steps. (I might also hold off grading it at all until the student writes more.)

How to Create a Rubric on Your Assignment Sheets

- Always use the same five categories: structure, process, description, spelling, and grammar.

- Beside each category, in parentheses list the skill(s) that you have introduced in the mini-lessons for the assignment.

- Add any other pertinent skills that students have learned in previous mini-lessons.

- If you run out of space, you can abbreviate, go on to a second line, or rotate some old skills out once most of the class has mastered them.

- Include a row marked TOTAL, and be sure to have two columns for a preliminary grade and a revised grade.

Preliminary Grade

When students first hand in a paper, even if it is nearly perfect, they should still be given a preliminary grade. Do not agonize over exactly how many points every single error (or revision) should be worth. Make it mathematically easy on yourself, and set a limit of five points per revision. (In a class that's really struggling, you could make it two points per revision.) So, if students get a paper back with a score of 15 for structure, they can deduce that they must revise one aspect of the paper's structure. If they receive five points for spelling, they know that they have spelled three words incorrectly. If students surpass four errors in any given category, I usually write a dash above the line rather than 0.

Sometimes, in a category such as description, deducting points can be a judgment call, but students never question me on it. Why? Because they know they can get every single point back with

> Using the rubric, you can emphasize the importance of prewriting by designating the points for a given task as the only points that cannot be earned back.

Student Note

"It helps me gain confidence back when I gain points back."
—*Natalie C.*

Writing Workshop in Middle School © 2013 by Marilyn Pryle • Scholastic

revision. In that way, it almost doesn't matter if I take off five or two or three points per revision, or if I assign a different point value to each revision. Students know it is only a preliminary grade, one meant to help them. During the first assignment, students are indeed surprised and a bit nervous to see their papers returned with numbers such as five and ten written on them, but after I reassure them of the system, and after they in fact see a higher revised grade on the second round, they relax and trust the process.

The only points a student cannot retrieve are points for prewriting. I stress this, reiterating that there is no right or wrong answer for a prewrite as long as one exists, and by definition it must be done *before* writing. If students hand in a completed paper without prewriting, they lose ten points permanently. I explain my reasoning: one cannot go back in time after the piece is written; it's not a *postwrite*. This is a sensible policy that emphasizes the importance of prewriting.

Revised and Final Grades

After students revise a paper based on the first round of grading, cross out the preliminary grade in each category and write in the new grade under the Revised Grade column. This new grade may or may not be a 20, since students often revise insufficiently. Because of this, I set 90 as a minimum grade for a paper to be called "finished." That is, students must revise their papers as many times as it takes to get a 90 or above. Obviously, you should do whatever you feel comfortable with here. A colleague of mine has 80 as his minimum finished grade; another has no minimum and lets students end where they want after their first revision. The thought of time spent grading compels me to ensure that students implement my suggestions. If we're all going to put in this much work, I want students to learn as much as possible. Their own writing is the most teachable material; only they can produce it. I don't want to let it go to waste. In addition, to an extent, I'm giving them the answers! Through my notes and individual conferencing, I make it perfectly clear what students must do to adequately revise their paper. Many students, even after receiving a 90, will revise again to 100, because they know they can. In this case, I add a new final column in the margin of the rubric.

Once students score a grade of 90, I write it on or near the TOTAL line and circle it. The circle is very important—a circled grade means students have clearance to file it in their finished folder. I do not total a grade before 90, although students will often total their own

---

Brainstorm It!

What will your minimum final grade be? Why?

---

grades out of curiosity or worry during the preliminary stages. I let them, as this can serve as a motivating factor for revision.

I have never had a problem with my administration, or within myself, giving many students *A*s during each quarter. Their portfolios speak for themselves, brimming with drafts and prewriting and revisions. The work is there. And at the same time, as most teachers know, not all students will take advantage of this system—unfortunately, despite my efforts, many of them do not finish all assignments or do not turn in some at all. I don't consider this class to be an easy *A*, and neither do the students. It's a reachable A, with effort.

As you can see, this system allows for plenty of room for your professional and individual judgment. At the same time, you'll have all the numbers you need to show students, their parents, and your principal.

The Act of Grading

I'll be honest about grading: it takes time. This is the nature of a workshop. The good news, however, is that with practice, you will become faster and more efficient as you read. In addition, the rubric will help you stay focused on the topics you have taught within each assignment. You will learn to let other errors and suggestions go—ones that do not yet correspond to the current assignment and its rubric. You will get better at recognizing what a paper needs and the order in which it is needed. All this will come! Be patient with yourself and with your students.

Usually, I circle grammar or spelling mistakes without any further notation. I want students to figure out their error—on their own or by using a reference source such as a book, the Internet, or a teaching poster. However, I've found that structural suggestions need to be written out. If the issue is too large to describe on paper, I'll write "See me" on the paper and a short note to myself to remind me what to discuss in a future conference. I try to write as much positive feedback as possible by highlighting specific accomplishments, such as "Strong intro," "Great trans. word," "Excellent semicolon!" or "Powerful example." And at the end of each paper, I always write a quick sentence or phrase that is encouraging. Even if the paper is rife with needed revisions, I'll write something positive such as, "Strong details so far—keep going!"

A paper that has been corrected once already does not take long to reread since the latest revision is always atop the earlier corrected copies, and all I have to do is flip between them. Reading revisions is actually quite rewarding: I am already familiar with the paper and do not have to wade through it, and I get a true sense of the student's understanding and progress. And most papers that come in for a third or fourth time require only a glance, since by then the student is fixing small spelling or grammatical errors. For clarity, I always use a pen of a different color for each new draft that a student hands in. This makes it easy to keep the drafts in order.

Grading Tip

Keep several different-colored pens nearby as you grade. With each paper, use a different color than you used on the draft below it. This will clarify the drafts and progress of the piece.

Writing Workshop in Middle School © 2013 by Marilyn Pryle • Scholastic

Grading Is Really About Revision

This grading system is not simply a way to evaluate student work; it is a tool to motivate students to revise. And revision, of course, is the heart of writing. I tell students this often, along with some quotes about revision from well-known authors, such as this one from Rita Dove: "In working on a poem, I love to revise. Lots of younger poets don't enjoy this, but in the process of revision I discover things." This is so true—I promise students that the thought they couldn't reach yesterday will be there the next day, or the next, if they give it time. I assure them that our brains are smarter than we think, and that the words come when we least expect them. Another reassuring thought comes from Robert Cormier: "The beautiful part of writing is that you don't have to get it right the first time, unlike, say, a brain surgeon." Naomi Shihab Nye echoes this when she says, "I see revision as a beautiful word of hope. It's a new vision of something. It means you don't have to be perfect the first time. What a relief!" I try to share my own passion for, and belief in, revision. In our fast-paced world, I want students to believe that it is worthwhile and meaningful to double back, to give attention, to wait for the right word to come.

> **Student Note**
>
> "Without the incentive of getting a better grade, the revision process isn't as in depth because it feels like there's no reason to revise."
>
> —Marissa Y.

How To Start Small

Here are some suggestions for starting the grading process:

- Start your first assignment or two with a rubric that contains the Process and Description categories. That way, you can make sure students are progressing through all the steps of an assignment (process) and are including what you taught in the first mini-lessons (such as lessons on banned words or sensory details, both of which would come under description). Then, gradually, add categories to your rubric.

- Use a more complete rubric but force yourself to only grade for *one* skill per category. For example, in structure only look for paragraph indentation; in description only look for sensory details; in grammar only look for periods at the ends of sentences. You could skip spelling for now. (*Note: Do grade for all process skills as you want students to get in the habit of the writing process.*)

- Grade spelling and grammar for only the first ten lines or so of any given assignment.

With whatever changes you make, feel free to adjust the points to your liking.

The Benefits of Attentive Grading

Grading indeed requires a good bit of your time, and a lot of your focus. Sifting through the words students have written attempting to determine what they are *trying* to say, and then figuring out how their words can better *say* it, is at times exhausting. However, I believe there is no better way to teach writing. Sentence exercises and limited prompts cannot come close. Students' own original thoughts, words, and sentences mean the most to them and tell the most to me. When I compare the papers at the end of the year with the papers from the beginning, and I see the growth that has taken place both intellectually and personally, I know the intensity of the work is worth it.

Writing Workshop in Middle School © 2013 by Marilyn Pryle • Scholastic

Chapter 8

Individual Conferencing: Talking to Students About Their Work

My favorite part of any workshop is conferencing with students one-on-one: listening to their explanations, watching them think, and even seeing a new idea take hold— it flashes in their eyes and raises their eyebrows in a moment of enthusiasm. Conferencing with my students is my chance to show my interest in all of their work and in each of *them*; it is a chance to connect with them on a level that can't be achieved during whole-group instruction.

Of course, this is not to say that students always feel the same way about conferencing with me. Sometimes they are reluctant, shy, embarrassed, or even annoyed—but that doesn't stop me from being excited by, or at least interested in, what they wrote. If I can get them to talk not just about the writing but also about the content of their work (which they of course chose and, therefore, think significant), it isn't long before they become engaged. What adolescent doesn't want genuine, encouraging interest from another person? My knowledge of their papers and desire to make their ideas stronger makes them feel worthy and important. Students quickly realize they have an audience who cares. They learn that writing—their writing—matters.

The more autonomous the class is as a whole, the more time you will have to give each student individually. If other students constantly interrupt your conference to ask where the highlighters are or what they should do when they finish an assignment, the conference will not be very productive or enjoyable. And although interruptions do happen in the first week or two of class, an early focus on making students self-sufficient will benefit everyone.

General Conference Guidelines

Below are some suggestions about how to most efficiently confer with students about their writing.

Silence

For a successful writer's workshop experience, students must work quietly in order for everyone to think. This is especially true when you are conferencing. If a student senses your distraction or annoyance during a conference, he or she may withdraw. Direct the class early on to work in silence, unless you have peer reading built into your system, which itself should be conducted using low voices. I tell students not to interrupt another student's conference with a question unless it is an emergency.

Be Ready!

Students often start chatting the minute they see you giving your full attention to a single student. Keep an ear out for this and be quick to remind the other students to keep working on their own.

Frequency

Class size obviously affects how often you can meet with your students. I like to conference, or at least check in, with each of my students every day. Most days, I am able to see students more than once because I usually keep the conferences relatively brief, and I also multiconference, both of which are described later. Some students may only need one conference per assignment; others may need more guidance. Some assignments are more difficult than others and require me to visit intensively with students for three consecutive days.

When to Conference?
After a mini-lesson, circulate around the room. A conference may arise because:
•   you have a graded paper to discuss with a student.
•   a student has a question.
•   you notice that someone is not working and needs direction.
•   you notice a student working but looking stuck.
•   you notice a student is transitioning from one phase to another (e.g., prewriting to drafting).

Writing Workshop in Middle School © 2013 by Marilyn Pryle • Scholastic

I do not have a set order for visiting students. After the mini-lesson, as the class settles in to its work, I might look for the most confused, frustrated, bored, or distracted student and begin there. Other times I might take that day's stack of corrected assignments and conference with each student as I return his or her paper. As I circulate I discuss the needed revisions; if the paper is finished with a final grade, I praise the student's efforts and ask what he or she is currently working on.

If students are clearly absorbed in writing, I generally won't disturb them, even if I have papers to return to them. I'll wait until later in the class, or even the next day. I know how valuable it is to be in the flow of writing!

Whenever I am circling the room, students can raise their hand for my help. Usually, the questions are brief, but they can serve as a springboard for a conference.

After I have seen all the students I will see for any given day, I return to my desk for a few minutes at the end of each class so students can approach me with additional questions. And desk time gives me a chance to get a small start on the grading for that day.

Conference Record-Keeping

If your class is small enough, you might not need to keep a record of which students you've conferenced with—you might be able to check in or conference with every student every day or every other day. However, if you have a larger class, or if you are new to individual conferencing with a large group, you may want to keep track of the students you've seen to ensure you've met with everyone at least once per assignment (this may take a few days). As for recording the content of the conferences, my belief is that it takes more effort and time than it's worth. I like to let the drafts speak for themselves. Often I will write notes in the margins of drafts when explaining certain concepts to students; these notes, and the revisions students make from draft to draft, serve as a record of the work.

Location

After the day's mini-lesson is over, I spend most of the class circulating around the room, returning papers, conferencing, answering questions, and maintaining discipline. In this mode, I conference with students wherever they are working. If they are at a computer, I take an empty seat beside them. If there isn't one, I'll just wait until later to talk to that student. When students are working at their desks, I sit at an empty nearby desk or pull over a chair from one of the computers. If there are too many other students around us, I might ask a student to come to my desk, but usually the class is spread around the room enough to provide sufficient space for me to conference desk-side. I like this method because it keeps students on their own "turf," and it seems less disruptive to them. It also reinforces my role as a coach, running out onto the field where the action is happening, instead of an all-knowledgeable leader whose subjects must come to her.

How to Keep Track of Individual Student Conferences

- Make an extra copy of your seating chart; as you conference, check off each student's name. Or abbreviate the day of the week next to each name as you conference so you will know exactly when you visited each student. Copy a new seating chart each week. Staple the seating charts for all your classes together and write the week's date on the front of the packet. This way, a quick glance will tell if you've seen each of your students at least once in a given week.

- Use a seating chart that has the weekdays listed under each student's name, and simply check off the day you see each student. Copy or print a new chart each week.

- Keep an alphabetical class chart for the entire quarter, split into weeks and days with dates on top. Check off the days you conference with individual students. Keep this chart exclusively to record your conferencing. Staple all your class charts together into a quarterly conferencing packet. (A copy is on page 158.)

Sample Conference Record Chart

CLASS:

M T W Th F	M T W Th F	M T W Th F	M T W Th F	M T W Th F	M T W Th F
M T W Th F	M T W Th F	M T W Th F	M T W Th F	M T W Th F	M T W Th F
M T W Th F	M T W Th F	M T W Th F	M T W Th F	M T W Th F	M T W Th F
M T W Th F	M T W Th F	M T W Th F	M T W Th F	M T W Th F	M T W Th F

I make it a point to always sit with students when we're conferencing. This may sound like a small detail, but I believe it goes a long way in setting the tone. When I sit down next to a student, I'm sending a message. I'm telling the student, I have some time to spend, I will give you my full attention, and for this moment, I have no where else to be. Standing and bending does not convey this impression; instead, it says I am on the move and only have a minute. Also, sitting puts me at eye level with students. Standing puts me above them, and squatting puts me below, which, I have found, tends to make students uncomfortable (not to mention my legs!).

Where to Conference?

If possible, sit with the student at his or her desk, using a nearby desk or chair. If the space is crowded, invite the student to your desk later.

Wherever the conference takes place, I want students to feel that at that moment, nothing is more important to me than the success of the piece and their growth as a writer and thinker. I go into every conference with that intention, and I want students to sense it.

Duration

I try to keep the conferences to about five minutes or less, in order to let students work. As much as students enjoy the individual attention, I don't think they want me sitting with them at their desks for fifteen minutes. Shorter conferences keep the momentum of the class flowing. They also allow me to circulate more and thus see more students, as well as maintain discipline. I must emphasize, however, that "shorter" does not mean "rushed." I keep a narrow focus—just one or two revisions at a time (see the later section on multiconferencing), although, when appropriate, a conference can exceed five minutes.

How Long to Conference?

Try to keep conferences short—five minutes or less. Address only one or two topics at a time.

Content

During a conference, I am willing to discuss anything that will help further the success of a piece of writing. At any given moment, I might act as detective, coach, instructor, psychiatrist, audience, archaeologist, cheerleader, or disciplinarian. The two main pillars of any conference, though, are praise and focus on meaning.

Praise

I always begin a conference with a positive comment. Sometimes this is easy to do; sometimes I have to search hard for a praiseworthy aspect. The comment cannot be faked though, not only because adolescents sense duplicity and loathe it, but more important, because I want to offer genuine encouragement. So I search. I'm not afraid to be silent at first, either reading what they have written or shuffling through drafts and notes. Students are used to watching me think in front of them. And without fail, I will find something, somewhere, to praise. Even in the worst-case scenario, when a student is sitting angrily in front of a single blank sheet of paper in total defiance, I can say something such as, "You wrote a wonderful ode a couple weeks ago; you're good at describing. I know you are perfectly capable of doing this assignment as well." I don't coddle students— they must always know that they are expected to work hard and thoughtfully—but honest, appropriate praise can go a long way in rejuvenating a stuck student, perking up an unmotivated student, or re-engaging a distracted student who is on the verge of misbehaving. With most papers, I can easily find something—a rich prewrite, a well-written intro, an original simile, a well-organized paragraph, *something*—that merits sincere appreciation. And the brief time it takes to offer praise is well worth it. Praise is a way for me to connect with my students, and it engages them even further into their writing. When they know that parts of their piece succeed, they are motivated to revise the parts that lag.

One notion I always avoid during conferences is talk of talent. Even if a student is so naturally gifted that there is little I can teach him or her, I refrain from saying, "Wow, you're so gifted" or "You have so much talent" or "You should think about becoming a professional writer." I will, on occasion, tell students who are struggling with their writing they are "a natural" at one technique or another, in order to boost confidence, but that kind of praise is extremely specific. I would never make a sweeping general comment about any student's overall ability, good or bad, during a writing conference, as this may discourage other students in the class or embarrass the targeted student. If anything, I might wait until a private conference at the end of the year to tell a student how talented I think he or she is.

Conferencing Tip

Address students by name during every conference. This simple habit does much to make the student feel connected to you and valued.

Focus on Meaning

When looking at a piece for the first time, I check to see if it's substantial enough to deal with as a draft. If not, my job is to help the student build it up from the inside out. If the draft seems sufficient, then I generally suggest revising from the outside in: first organization, then details, and then grammar. I resist the urge to fix (or have the student fix) all the little grammar mistakes as I read. It is a waste of energy for me to focus on conventions early on in a piece unless the muddled grammar obscures meaning to the point of confusion. Students often correct something on their own in the middle of the conference; this is natural. But for me to dive into the grammatical issues of a piece at the beginning of a conference dampens students' momentum and enthusiasm. Writers write in order to say something meaningful, and if I bypass the meaning in favor of perfecting the grammar, students are apt to feel discouraged and even slighted.

Conferencing Tip

When you see a draft for the first time, resist correcting every single grammatical mistake! Instead, check to see if enough content exists, and then look at the main ideas and organization.

That said, I do not necessarily wait until the final conference to talk about grammar. Often it will come up once the process of revising the details, organization, tone, and such is under way. Once I have students confidently revising one aspect of their draft, I will mention a pattern of grammatical mistakes that needs attention. Although meaning trumps grammar in the initial conferences, grammar is not insignificant; it is merely secondary. Also, the number of grammar mistakes plays a role. If a student has mangled the use of every mark of punctuation after we've gone over the other aspects of the piece, I will do a full lesson on punctuation. However, if a student only missed one apostrophe, I will wait until the student hands in the paper and circle the spot so he or she can figure it out independently. And if, say, a mild pattern of switching verb tense appears in the paper, I will mention it while we're discussing other revisions, as described above.

Writing Workshop in Middle School © 2013 by Marilyn Pryle • Scholastic

General Progression of What to Look for in a Draft

Figure out where the student is in his or her writing, and do only one of these at a time. In addition, don't feel like you must have a conference for each step—this is just a general guideline of how to approach a student's draft. All categories referenced beside "NO" can be found in the Some Conferencing Techniques section at the end of this chapter.

1. The student has written a first draft.	→ NO	See "Nothing to Write."

YES ↓

2. Is the draft substantial enough to count as draft?	→ NO	See "Adding Content/ Elaboration."

YES ↓

3. (For essays): Is there a clear thesis? Does it have a main idea?	→ NO	See "Thesis."

YES (or N/A) ↓

4. (For narrative): Is there a point to the piece, a deeper meaning?	→ NO	See "Theme."

YES ↓

5. Is the draft reasonably well organized?	→ NO	See "Organization."

YES ↓

6. Is there enough elaboration of details, reasons, and examples?	→ NO	See "Details" and "Adding Content/Elaboration."

YES ↓

7. Is the language strong and exciting?	→ NO	See "Language."

YES ↓

8. Is the introduction engaging and clear?	→ NO	See "Introduction."

YES ↓

9. Is the conclusion interesting and somehow *new*?	→ NO	Revisit "Theme" and see "Other Conclusions/Clinchers."

YES ↓

10. Is the title informative and interesting?	→ NO	See "Titles."

YES ↓

11. Are all conventions correct?	→ NO	See "Conventions and Spelling."

YES ↓

TELL THE STUDENT TO HAND IN THE DRAFT!

If a student's paper is saturated with every imaginable grammatical error, we first work on developing the piece as a whole. Usually in these cases, the major aspects of the piece—the details, theme, and organization—will also need major improvements. Then I'll choose one or two grammatical topics to focus on. In the student's next assignment, we can move to the next point in grammar.

Overall, I enjoy helping students master the conventions of our language. It empowers them. With grammar, I try to take the tone of a teammate rather than a teacher, acknowledging when the rules of grammar are difficult or even illogical, while communicating my belief in students' ability to grasp them.

Multiconferencing

Multiconferencing might be the most useful conferencing technique of the workshop. Here are some of its benefits:

- It breaks down the revising process into specific, manageable parts for students.
- Students don't feel the pressure of being watched as they work.
- You can visit many students during one class period.
- Constantly circulating enables you to ensure that students keep working and helps prevent discipline problems.

Multiconferencing, which incorporates aspects of both content and duration, looks like this:

1. Visit a student, assess what his or her draft most immediately needs, and discuss the draft with the student, initially focusing on what will most help the draft overall. Then give the student one or two small, concrete tasks to do in order to reach that immediate goal. When you are sure the student understands your instructions, explain that you will check back after a few minutes after the student has had a chance to work independently.

2. Repeat Step 1 with two or more students.

3. If the first student is still working, repeat Steps 2 and 3. Otherwise, check back on the first student. If the draft is ready to be handed in, direct the student to do so. If not, figure out what the draft still needs, and give the student another task or two. Move on to another student.

4. Continue visiting new students while periodically checking with students you've already visited.

The key to efficient multiconferencing is that you give students small, manageable tasks that they can do on their own. They don't need you to sit there, which frees you up to see more students. In this way, class time becomes a chain of productivity.

Writing Workshop in Middle School © 2013 by Marilyn Pryle • Scholastic

What is a small, meaningful, concrete task?

Depending on what a draft needs (see the chart on page 109), a small task can range from making lists of sensory details to getting a pair of scissors and cutting all the draft paragraphs apart and rearranging them like a puzzle. Your instructions need to be specific. You wouldn't say, "Your conclusion needs work" and walk away. Instead, you would say, "Think of three possible solutions to the problem you present in your thesis. Write each one down."

Examples of Small, Concrete Tasks

Here are some more examples of small, concrete tasks, although really the possibilities are endless:

- List the five senses on the student's paper and tell him or her to write three details about the setting under each sense.

- With the student, identify the essay's three main ideas and then color-code those ideas with different-colored highlighters. Then have the student highlight each sentence in the coordinating color. (A rainbow will indicate a lack of organization!) When you return, help the student reorganize the essay.

- Review what a linking verb is and have the student underline all the linking verbs in his or her paper. When you return to check with the student, have him or her change six of those linking verbs to action verbs.

- Put asterisks next to three places in a student's paper where a transition word is needed, and send the student to the Transition Words poster to see which word would best fit.

- Have the student list the three most important ideas or moments from his or her paper. When you return, underline any words from this list that you find powerful, then direct the student to write two possible titles using some of the words you underlined.

- Underline any repeated mistake related to conventions. Explain the convention to the student and leave him or her to fix all the underlined words independently.

Notice that these suggestions involve a specific number of tasks, the underlining of certain words or phrases, or choosing from a poster or the student's own list. This is what makes the tasks concrete and manageable. I don't just say to a student, "Put in more sensory details." I instruct the student to list three details under each of the five senses. That writer may not use all fifteen details, but he or she will have plenty to choose from. Likewise, I don't simply instruct a student to "show, don't tell" and leave him or her to figure out what that means; neither do I simply direct the student to "add transition words." I make sure to indicate where these transition words should go and suggest transition words to choose from.

Tips for Giving Small, Concrete Tasks During Conferences

Here are some general tips for devising small, concrete tasks during conferences:

- If possible, put a number on a task. This gives the student an end goal.

- Try to limit each visit to one topic (details, linking verbs, transition words, and so on). This keeps students focused without overwhelming them. If there are no larger or repeated issues to address, combine two small topics at most.

- Make categories for the student to create lists under (five senses, pros/cons, three statistics).

- Involve other resources: posters, different-colored pens or highlighters, scissors, other books, and so on. (I once had a student read the first line of every short story in her English anthology and create categories of first-line techniques.)

- If possible, set up choices for the student. For example, have him or her list ten sensory details and then choose seven of them. Or have the student write out two possible attention-grabbers (e.g., a statement of general truth and a statistic) and let him or her choose a favorite.

Consider the example below. Colleen, an eighth grader, has written an autobiographical account about guiding a woman and her son off thin ice at a local pond. Colleen's essay begins like this:

I'm a Junior Hockey Patrol, one of the people who tests the ice at our pond, Ice Pond. If the ice is too thin, I must put up the "Danger, Thin Ice" signs. On this particular day, it was windy, but not bitter cold. As I enter the area around the pond, I notice a small boy pushing stacked crates around the ice.

Colleen and I have already met about the overall structure of the piece and its theme, both of which are in good shape. I feel we can continue with a discussion of the introduction.

Writing Workshop in Middle School © 2013 by Marilyn Pryle • Scholastic

Ms. P.: Colleen, as I told you before, this is a wonderful story—you are so brave!

Colleen: Yeah, we get trained for the worst-case scenarios, but you never think you're going to have to use them, you know?

Ms. P.: I know. OK, now, we've met a couple times already, and the story is shaping up nicely. Your theme is clear, and you have interesting details throughout. Great job so far.

Colleen: Thanks.

Ms. P.: Let's look at your intro. You give us some helpful background information, and I like how you end the paragraph with the conflict—the boy on the ice. However, it's not exactly an attention-grabber. I think you need more details. (*I purposefully use the word* conflict, *and assume that Colleen strategically introduced this element where she did.*)

Colleen: OK.

Ms. P.: Here's what I'm thinking: can you put us right into the moment of either standing at the pond or approaching the pond? You have a detail here about the wind—"it was windy." That's good to point out, but instead of just *telling* us it was windy, can you *show* us? Remember how I'm always saying, "Show, don't tell?" It's just an expression that means a writer should describe the wind using sensory details, in your case, instead of simply saying, "It was windy" and expecting the reader to believe you based on your word. Do you know what I mean?

Colleen: I think so—I should give an example of wind.

Ms. P.: Exactly. Here's a tip-off that you're telling and not showing: you use the verb *was*. It's called a linking verb—do you remember that mini-lesson? Linking verbs include *am, is, was, were, being,* and *been,* and they don't convey any action. They're like equal signs. A linking verb means you're telling. If you use a verb with action, an active verb, you're showing. At any rate, showing the wind might make an interesting introduction. And feel free to add any other sensory details that you can think of. Then you can give the background information after. (I write "Senses—sights, sounds, smells, textures" at the top of her paper as I am speaking.)

Colleen: OK. So I should move what I have now to the middle of the paragraph and start with some new sentences?

Ms. P.: Exactly. Start in the moment to get the reader's attention and fill in the background info after. I'll check back.

I leave Colleen to figure out which sensory detail to use to craft an attention-grabbing introduction. While she is working, I visit another student or two. Also, notice in this example that I began the conference with praise and that I was able to work in a grammar mini-lesson.

When students successfully finish a small task, they feel a sense of accomplishment and gain confidence to move forward. Also, in revisiting students several times, I get frequent opportunities to encourage them and praise their work. Multiconferencing ensures that students work more, drafts improve steadily and incrementally, and the atmosphere stays positive and productive.

Sample Conferences

I'd like to present a few scenarios that can arise during a conference and how I like to handle them. These conversations will illustrate some of the tenets described above.

Conference #1: Finding a Theme

Students often learn to generate wonderful details, organize clear paragraphs, and craft interesting introductions before they fully grasp the idea of theme. It can take time before students come to realize that theme is not about creating a maxim on life but about linking their experience to the universal human experience. With each assignment, I work with every student to understand the themes in his or her own work. This aspect illustrates the effectiveness of writing workshop: Instead of studying concepts like theme from the outside in (as in a literature class), students experience it from the inside out.

I use several techniques and questions to help the student uncover the theme of the piece. Often, students reveal truths in their writing that are not immediately apparent to themselves; my job is to help them look deeper into their memories and thoughts to locate these profound ideas.

Below is a conversation I had with Ashlyn regarding her character sketch about her sister, Kate. Ashlyn obviously admired her older sister tremendously: She listed a myriad of precise details about Kate's appearance and habits, along with many of her achievements. However, the sketch had another dimension to it: a scene in which Kate was so busy studying, and then getting a phone call, that she didn't have time to help Ashlyn with her homework. Ashlyn was struggling with a way to end the sketch, having written to the point where she was standing outside Kate's door, frustrated and waiting for her sister to get off the phone.

Ms. P.:	How's it going Ashlyn?
Ashlyn:	OK, I guess. It was easy thinking of details, but now I don't know how to end it.
Ms. P.:	Let's see what you have here. (*I read over the sketch.*) This is excellent. I love how you describe her "pink pajama bottoms" and "brown, shoulder length, layered hair." (*I star these sentences on her draft as I read them.*) Great details!
Ashlyn:	Thanks.
Ms. P.:	An easy way to end a character sketch is with a theme—do you remember how to do that?
Ashlyn:	You mean why the person is important to me?
Ms. P.:	Yes. Also, ask yourself what have you learned from Kate, about yourself or about life.
Ashlyn:	I thought about that, and I think I already have it in the first sentence.

Writing Workshop in Middle School © 2013 by Marilyn Pryle • Scholastic

The seventeen year old that I call my sister is so photogenic, artistic, smart and stylish that I can't help just wanting to be like her. "Um . . . hey, Kate?" I asked while poking my head through her bedroom door, in an unsure voice, not sure if she was in a likable mood today.

Ms. P.: You do have her good qualities there, and I wouldn't change it—I like that as a beginning. But look what you have at the end of that paragraph. Is she sometimes in bad moods?

Ashlyn: Well, she's just so busy, sometimes she doesn't like me bothering her.

Ms. P.: Yes, I see that the sketch is about that. So maybe you should think about how she has two sides to her, how people can be complex . . .

Ashlyn: Sometimes I think about how she's under a lot of pressure all the time.

Ms. P.: OK, good. So, in the beginning of the sketch, you want to be just like her . . . but maybe everything doesn't come so easy as it seems for her.

Ashlyn: That's just it—she seems perfect but she's just human. (*I write down "seems perfect—just human" at the bottom of Ashlyn's draft.*)

Ms. P.: Good! See what you can do with that—it could be a really sophisticated ending, Ashlyn, really mature. Give it a try, and I'll check on you in a bit.

Ashlyn: OK.

When I check back, Ashlyn has added the following two paragraphs to the end of her draft.

I was getting so bored waiting outside Kate's door. But then it occurred to me, "What would it be like to be Kate?" I thought of how hard it was for her to do all her homework, write a bunch of college essays, go to her job, and find time for her friends and fun. Then on top of that, she's always helping my mother clean and me with my homework.

I realized it wasn't easy for Kate being herself. She's not perfect, but she's perfect in a way. She has so many goals in life, and she has managed to get to them. She takes on any challenge and I really admire her for that.

Ms. P.: Ashlyn, this is really good. You made her, and yourself, more complex—like a real person! This is what writers aim for, to capture life like it really is.

Ashlyn: Thanks.

Ms. P.: Now let's look at the very end. You have the theme—but what about a last sentence that will really stick with the reader?

Ashlyn: How?

Ms. P.: Well, one trick that usually works is to go back to the moment. (*I give this advice to students all the time—they often want to generalize their way out of a piece of writing, but sticking with the moment is so much more satisfying.*) Where were you when we last saw you?

Ashlyn: Um, standing outside Kate's door.

Ms. P.: OK. What normally happens next? Does she come out? Do you just walk away? How do you feel in this scene after you thought about her?

Ashlyn: I was trying to be patient. (*I write "patient" on her draft.*) She will usually come and find me when she has time.

Ms. P.: All right—that's a lot to work with. Can you just add one or two sentences at the very end, putting us back at your sister's door? I think that would really clinch it. Try starting a sentence with the word *as*, like, "As I stood outside her door . . ." (*I write this on her draft. I often start a complex sentence for students as a model.*)

Ashlyn: OK. I'll try.

Her final ending appears below.

> *I realized it wasn't easy for Kate being herself. She's not perfect, but she's perfect in a way. She has so many goals in life, and she has managed to get to them. She takes on any challenge and I really admire her for that. As I stood outside her bedroom door, I promised to be more patient with her. A little later, she came to my room and was ready to help. She always has time for me in the end.*

Conference #2: Tightening up Language

When a student reaches a point in a draft where the main ideas, theme, organization, and details are mostly in place, I try to help with language. In this next example, Dave has written an analysis of the poem "Bereft" by Robert Frost.

Bereft

Where had I heard this wind before
Change like this to a deeper roar?
What would it take my standing there for,
Holding open a restive door,
Looking down hill to a frothy shore?
Summer was past and the day was past.
Sombre clouds in the west were massed.
Out on the porch's sagging floor,
Leaves got up in a coil and hissed,
Blindly struck at my knee and missed.
Something sinister in the tone
Told me my secret must be known:
Word I was in the house alone
Somehow must have gotten abroad,
Word I was in my life alone,
Word I had no one left but God.

Writing Workshop in Middle School © 2013 by Marilyn Pryle • Scholastic

Dave has a solid understanding of the poem, and the main ideas of his middle paragraphs are about the title, tone, and rhyme scheme. At first his paragraph on tone looks like this:

There is another thing in the poem that will help the reader understand how the feeling of the poem is. It is the tone. By these next couple of quotes you will definitely see why the tone of this poem is sad. The first is "sombre clouds in the west were massed." Another example of the world being against him is "out on the porch's sagging floor." Which is basically saying how everything he sees has something bad about it. Nothing in his life is good anymore.

Ms. P.: Dave, you did such a good job writing about this poem. You back up all of your claims with quotes, and you really hit upon the feeling of loss in the poem. Great work!

Dave: Thanks.

Ms. P.: Let's just take a look at some places where you can strengthen the language and cut some words. Remember what I'm always saying to class about using fewer words?

Dave: Um, that less words is better?

Ms. P.: Right—using fewer, stronger words is better than a lot of words that don't say a lot. So you always want to try to say the same idea but with fewer words.

Dave: OK.

Ms. P.: Look at your third paragraph about the tone of the poem. What am I going to tell you about the word "thing"?

Dave: Oh yeah. It's banned. I forgot. So I should say, "point" or "characteristic" or something like that?

Ms. P.: Well, maybe, but let's see . . . a lot of times using banned words means you're also using too many words. Tell me this. What is the definition of "tone"? (*I underline it in his second sentence.*)

Dave: Um . . . the feeling of the poem?

Ms. P.: Right—the feeling of the speaker. And you say that in the first sentence. So basically, you're saying the "thing" that will help readers understand the feeling of the poem is the tone, when tone is the feeling of the poem. See how you're repeating?

Dave: Oh . . . yeah, I do.

Ms. P.: Now look at your third sentence. See any word that shouldn't be there?

Dave: Umm . . .

Ms. P.: It rhymes with "who."

Dave: Oh! "You." I missed that one.

> Sometimes, the solution to eradicating banned words is not simply replacing the word with another but trimming the entire sentence.

Ms. P.:	Yes, I see you changed all the other "you's" in the paper, which was great. But look at what you're doing here—you're telling the reader what will happen instead of just showing the reader the quote. Don't tell us what you're going to do . . .
Dave:	Right. Just do it.
Ms. P.:	Good. So the only part of that third sentence that's important is the end. What are you saying there?
Dave:	That the tone is sad.
Ms. P.:	Excellent. Here's what I want you to do. Combine the first three sentences in this paragraph. You're really only making one main point here. I want you to use the words *tone* and *sad*. (*I circle "tone" and "sad" in his draft.*) I also want you to use the word "images." (*I write this in the margin.*) See what you can come up with. (*I resist writing the sentence for him!*) I'll be back to check.
Dave:	OK.

Dave combined the sentences into this sentence:

The tone of the poem is sad and the reader can see this in the images.

Other parts of the paragraph need fixing—the fragment, the other banned words—but I will point these out when I grade the paper in writing. I've used the brief conference time to focus closely on only three sentences, but hopefully Dave will remember the lesson and try to condense as he writes.

Some Conferencing Techniques

In General

- Dictate back students' actual spoken words; write down anything usable students say.
- Soften criticism with terms such as "a bit," "somewhat," or "a little," without backing away from the issue.
- Let students know when they have more knowledge about a hobby, place, sport, or area of study than you do.
- Repeatedly point out what real writers do and acknowledge when students employ those habits. Always treat students as real writers and refer to them as such.
- Break up instruction with questions or by having students list, underline, highlight, circle, checkmark, count, or read aloud.
- Don't dumb down literary terms; instead, phrase them so that students will understand their meaning through context.

Writing Workshop in Middle School © 2013 by Marilyn Pryle • Scholastic

Nothing to Write

- Connect to sample reading.
- Review students' Topics for Writing list.
- Ask students to make short lists for categories that you name.
- Get students talking—help them find an emotional connection to a topic.

Adding Content/Elaboration

- Check students' brainstorming—see if anything there could be expanded upon.
- Pick out one moment, place, person, or object and help students add sensory details about that.
- Narrow down the action (Yes, narrow!) to a smaller moment, and add sensory details; assure students that a single moment can be described in a complete paper.
- Ask students questions—get them talking about the topic and jot down words and phrases they use on their paper.
- Divide what students have to do into three or four groups and tell them that each group must add three details/examples/facts and so on. (You are spreading out their ideas and asking them to go deeper into those ideas.)
- Give students a certain number of elements to add: two examples per paragraph, four sensory details per paragraph, and so on.
- Get students talking to help them find an emotional connection to a topic.

Thesis (for non-narrative essays)

- Have students explain in their own words how they feel about a topic; repeat it back and have them take notes.
- Give students key phrases of a potential thesis (particular to their topic and opinion) and let them piece the sentence together.
- Ask students what they think the main idea is; write it down at the top of the paper, and then skim through it together, judging if their other thoughts fit with the main idea or not—and suggest they either cut extra thoughts or revise the main idea as they go.

Details

- List the five senses.
- Require a specific number of details or a certain length of freewriting.
- Remind students there are no incorrect details, only ones they will use and ones they won't.

- Underline "telling" sentences and have students convert them to "showing" sentences; tell students not to use the telling word but make sure, through description, the reader will be thinking it.
- Have students convert linking verbs to action verbs.
- Ask about existing details to find additional or more specific details; for example, for sight details, ask about colors; for sounds, onomatopoeia.

Theme

- Look for a hint of a theme in students' details, phrasing, and plot.
- Have students begin a sentence with "I learned," "I realized," or "I knew then."
- Ask students, "How did you change from this experience?"
- Say, "It's not just about [the student's topic], it's about your life. [The topic] is a part of your life, don't you think?"

Organization

Before students write:

- Prevent disorganization by giving detailed instructions on what types of organizational scaffolds work best for each genre.
- Draw attention to organizational possibilities by having students analyze sample essays for each genre.

During and after writing:

- Check students' prewriting.
- Help students sort out a few main ideas, make an outline, and cut the rest.
- List some transition words in an order that would fit students' essays and have them structure their paragraphs around them.
- Have students physically cut the draft paragraphs apart, then arrange the ideas in order, tape them to a new page, or save in envelopes.
- Tell students to assign a highlighting color to each main idea and then highlight the entire essay in those colors; review the results with students.

Introduction

- Look for the moment of best description or tension; tell students to start there, and use flashback to fill in.
- Encourage students to examine the first paragraphs in an anthology of short stories.
- Compile a file or binder of finished essays and let students examine their introductions.

Writing Workshop in Middle School © 2013 by Marilyn Pryle • Scholastic

- Create a poster called "Ways to Start an Essay," hang it in the classroom, and refer to it often.
- Determine where the bulk of the essay's information gathers, or where students' interest in the topic is most clear, and see if one of the approaches can be used in relation to that.
- Have students write two or three introductions and analyze them.

Other Conclusions/Clinchers (Besides a Theme)

- Keep students grounded in the specifics; don't let them pull back into generalities. (This is different from using the technique of a general statement of truth, which should apply directly and specifically to the essay's theme.)
- Look for a specific image in the paper that can be saved for the end or reused, this time with symbolism.
- Revisit the examples in the piece and dig deeper; the new ideas can be incorporated in the conclusion.
- Suggest a specific sentence construction (such as *If . . . then* or *Not only . . . but also*); even start the sentence for students and let them fill in the rest.

Language

- Check for banned words (*good, bad, things, great, stuff, sort of, kind of*).
- Give students one or two alternatives to a banned or weak word, ask them to add a third and then choose one.
- Constantly direct students toward sensory details.
- Help students eradicate linking verbs.
- Remind students not to start sentences the same way in the same paragraph.
- Direct students to sources (posters, thesauri, sample essays or poems, and so on) for ideas.
- Find words such as *something, someone, somewhere*, and so on. Ask: *Should it be named?*
- Look for two or more words whose meaning can be conveyed in one word.
- Be aware of verb-adverb combinations whose meaning can be conveyed in a single, stronger verb.
- Look for verb-preposition combinations.
- Pare large chunks of passive voice by looking for the doers of the actions.

Titles

- Give students key words from their piece that symbolize or indicate the theme and topic. Have students mix and match them to form titles.
- Remind students of their thesis.
- Search for vital information in the piece that can be extracted to create the title (for example, a place name).

Conventions and Spelling

- See if an error is repeated and start there; when explaining it, write down an additional example at the bottom of the page so students have it for reference.
- Send students to a teaching poster for reference (see Chapter 5 for poster ideas).
- For a paper with an assortment of editing errors, circle only five and see if students can figure out the errors on their own; check back to see how they did, and then circle another five (if needed).
- If necessary, copy or print a short exercise from a grammar book or the Internet and give it to students for extra practice on a certain topic.

Revising Poetry

- Push for the most specific detail possible.
- Trim any words that can be cut.
- Look for any unconsciously repeated words and change or cut them.
- Envision the poem in another form (stanzas or no stanzas) and suggest students play with the lines on a computer and observe the effect.
- Examine the line breaks. Students can keep to the rule of a line being 1) meaningful and 2) interesting, or they can break it somewhere unexpected for effect. Suggest places where students can experiment with line breaks on the computer.
- Look for a phrase where repetition might be effective.
- Punctuation should be appropriate—no commas at the end of every line.
- Is there an interesting word in the poem that students can look to rhyme?

Ending a Poem

- Stay in the moment.
- Try a simile.
- Look at the lines preceding the weak ending: Is there anything there that can be expanded into a better ending?

Writing Workshop in Middle School © 2013 by Marilyn Pryle • Scholastic

- Can the final lines simply be cut and earlier lines be used as an ending?
- Is there an overarching image in the poem, or a small detail that can be used in an interesting way at the end?
- Can repetition be used?

✳ ✳ ✳

Regardless of the topic during a conference, my underlying message conveys confidence in the students. I expect and assume they are trying their best. My ultimate goal is always to help them improve. They will not all end up writing with the same voice, nor will they be mini-versions of me. But I believe that all of them can grow as writers and thinkers and that their lives will be richer for it. This conviction leads me to approach students to discuss which parts of their minds, hearts, and lives they have put on paper for me to read.

Chapter 9

Writing and the World: Test-Taking and Publishing

There comes a time when the world knocks on the door of the insulated little sanctuary of the writing workshop, or when a piece of writing becomes so mature that it must fly out. Here I address how we, as writers, meet the world.

Test-Taking

Essay writing is the presumed genre for most standardized tests at the middle school level, but if the standardized test in your state uses a different genre, or if you teach the lower grades, the concepts here still apply.

Sometime at the beginning of the year or when I give the first essay assignment (this can vary depending on the grade and curriculum), I spend some class time exploring the concept of genre and trying to answer the question "What is an essay?" Students usually get a quick lesson on the meaning of the word *genre* when they label their assignment log for their finished folders. To begin to dig deeper, I write "genre" on the board, and before I can ask anything, someone usually tries to pronounce it: "Jen-ry? What's that?" It's from the French, I explain, and pronounce it for them. Some students realize they have heard it before; one might even remember its meaning. I expound and use music as an example, offering categories such as classical, punk, and swing. Soon hands shoot up with the musical genres they know: pop, alternative, rap, hip-hop, hard rock, ska (I had to have this term explained to me), and I know they've got the concept.

I then ask what writing genres they know. Most classes immediately list poetry and fiction (they may say "short stories" and "novels"). I help them organize terms such as *autobiography*, *biography*, and *essays* under the umbrella of nonfiction. Someone may even volunteer "script" or "play," since we have a dramatic adaptation of *The Diary of Anne Frank* in our eighth-grade curriculum. Someone may even add "newspaper article" and "letter." I list all of these and circle "essay." This, I explain, is what we will focus on.

One of the most effective ways of defining a concept is to explore what it's not. On the board, I outline a giant chart with columns labeled Essays, Fiction, Poems, and Plays. Students duplicate the chart in their notebooks and record the information in their tables of contents. I ask them to think of characteristics that are specific to each genre (this eliminates answers such as "it uses words") and list them. Then we discuss their thoughts and develop a master list on the board, which usually resembles the chart below:

ESSAYS	FICTION	POEMS	PLAYS
• explain something about real people • author's opinion • true • describe something • short (1–2 pages) • introduction/ conclusion	• made-up characters • plot • theme • not true • a lot of description • short or long • chapters	• rhyming • sometimes short • short lines • sometimes like a puzzle • similes • can be about any topic • stanzas	• dialogue without quotes • stage directions • meant to be acted • not much description • instructions for actors • split into acts

I elicit some of these ideas by using student answers from another category. For example, if someone claims that plays don't have much description, I ask if any other genres might typically use a lot of description. I should also note that I let certain generalities slide, such as the idea that poems are always short or rhyming, for the sake of time and the overall comparison. Or I modify the idea by adding words such as *can* or *sometimes*, as in "can be short" or "sometimes rhymes."

By now students can see how essays differ from other genres. "But look at the essay column," I suggest to the class. "It seems that there can be different types of essays—genres within a genre." I help students convert the ideas on the chart into actual essay genres: explanatory, biography/autobiography, persuasive, descriptive.

There are even more types of essays than these, I explain, and we will be learning about them throughout the year. I ask, "Looking at this preliminary list, however, what are some characteristics that *all* essays share? Look at our original chart for help." I want the class to realize that all essays are nonfiction. I add that essays are written from the author's point of view. This is easy to see with persuasive essays, I say, but it is true with other essays as well: The author's voice comes through clearly. Then we create a definition of the essay in our own words: *Essay—a usually short piece of nonfiction written from the author's perspective.*

I always like to add that the word *essay* can be used as a verb, meaning "to try." (I emphasize the shift in pronunciation.) I explain that the root of *essay* is "to weigh," meaning to weigh something in one's mind, to test it out, to examine it from different angles. Imagine holding an idea in your mind the way you would hold an apple in your hand, I tell them, turning it, feeling its weight, looking at its color, deciding if it's good enough to eat.

Sample Essays

One of the most effective ways to demonstrate how to score well on an essay test is to show students sample essays from each scoring category. These essays may be generated by test makers (or teachers) or, better yet, may be actual student essays that have been published by the state or testing company. Some states post sample essays on their Web sites or provide study guides that include sample essays. Showing students copies of these essays will greatly enhance their understanding of what is expected of them. For example, in Massachusetts, the middle school essays are given scores ranging from 1–6. Student essays representing each scoring category appear on the state's Web site. I create sets of these, and give each student a set to peruse.

Before students examine these essays, I distribute a copy of the corresponding essay question and give each student a chart for scoring the essays.

SAMPLE ESSAYS

	1	2	3	4	5	6
STRONG						
WEAK						

We begin by reading the prompt. Then we read the lowest-scoring essay as a class. Students then take a few minutes to note its strong and weak points on their chart. As we review their responses, students must add any new ideas from classmates to their own chart. We do the same for all the essays. By reading six essays that answer the same question, students can clearly see which skills are rewarded and which mistakes cause deductions. One year, our chart looked like this:

Writing Workshop in Middle School © 2013 by Marilyn Pryle • Scholastic

	1	2	3	4	5	6
STRONG		• main idea exists but vague	• main idea • paragraphs • two examples • grammar mostly OK	• clear main idea • three examples w/details • paragraphs w/ some transition words • grammar & sp. OK	• clear main idea • clear examples (3) w/details • 3 pgs. long • few grammar/sp. mistakes • good trans. wds. • strong vocab. • good intro.	• clear and interesting main idea • full 4 pgs. • almost no grammar/sp. mistakes • excellent vocab. • transition words in every par. • examples explained fully • clever intro. • strong conclusion
WEAK	• very short (1/4 page!) • no main idea • no examples • poor sp., vocab., & grammar	• too short (1 page) • barely one example • poor sp., vocab., & grammar	• examples should have more detail • many sp. errors • easy vocab. and banned words	• easy vocab. and banned words • details could be fuller • boring intro. • conclusion is just repeating	• conclusion is repeating	

While most states publicize charts illustrating how the essays are scored, I find it much more effective to have students compare the essays and deduce for themselves precisely which skills are rewarded at each point level. One element of the higher-scored essays that becomes apparent to students during this exercise is that length counts. Full paragraphs with examples are a must. The state chart won't say, "Length counts!" Instead it uses more sophisticated terminology, such as, "idea development" and "rich topic," which students may or may not understand. Length does not automatically equal a rich topic, of course; my point is that students will learn much more from their own analysis and paraphrasing of the scoring system than from reading a state-issued list.

If your state does not provide sample essays, it should at least supply schools with the criteria for each score. I would suggest taking this criteria and generating your own essays for students to compare.

Practice Questions

Writing responses to practice questions is effective test preparation. Having students do a dress rehearsal of sorts using sample essay questions issued by the state often serves to deliver a tremendous boost confidence and lower anxiety. As much as you can, make sure they know exactly what to expect, from the question format to the page layout to the amount of writing space provided on the test. Take this information directly from your state's preparation materials.

Test formats vary from state to state. Massachusetts requires middle school students to write a persuasive essay. On the test, the main question is preceded by an introduction at the top of the page. Students then have four pages of blank paper for a rough draft, followed by four lined pages for a final copy. All of this is provided in the state's preparation materials. I instruct students to brainstorm and group ideas on the question page, then to do as much crossing out and rewriting as they want on the rough draft pages, and finally, to write neatly on the final draft pages.

Show students as many sample and past questions as you can find. Read them all; have students brainstorm and group a few, and fully write out essays for one or two, depending on how many days you can devote to the practice.

Acronyms

Acronyms are some of the oldest mnemonic aids, perhaps because they work so well. I try to invent some before test time to help students remember what they've learned. Two that I use are "By Gosh It's Cold!" and "VEST." The first stands for _Brainstorm, Group, Introduction,_ and _Conclusion_: the four main structural elements in essay writing. The second stands for _Verbs, Examples, Sentences,_ and _Transition_ words. The Verbs category includes verb upgrading and tense continuity. The Sentence category refers to sentence variation as well as run-ons and fragments.

Another acronym I use for older students is "4 BITES." This means they should aim to

Writing Workshop in Middle School © 2013 by Marilyn Pryle • Scholastic fill up the full four pages (or however many pages are provided) with their essay—again, not because length automatically counts, but because when students write more, they are more likely to write something meaningful that adds to their essay. "BITES" stands for *Brainstorm, Introduction, Thesis, Examples,* and *Spell it out!* ("Spell it out" doesn't refer to spelling but to elaboration.)

Whatever students can remember from any of the letters is a bonus, so I try not to raise anxiety levels by drilling them too hard on the acronyms. I tell myself to trust in the process and the work we've done all year.

Revisiting Audience and Tone

Remind students that they have a very specific audience for the test: adult readers, many of them English teachers. They should remember to be careful with their tone and avoid using a sarcastic or an angry voice. Students who resent having to take the test should not let their feelings seep into their essays. Sometimes, one of the lower-scoring sample essays uses a negative tone, which can help you demonstrate the point. Emphasize to your students that test graders did not invent the test; they are just interested in students' writing skills. If students want to protest the test, they should do so in the form of a letter for social change sent to the appropriate recipients.

Checking Your Own Tone

Making sure that you stay calm, confident, and positive in the weeks prior to testing time can only benefit students. Try to convert any anxiety or negativity you may have into something positive. Try not to pass on the pressure that teachers feel at testing time. I remind myself that good can come out of testing; namely, the existence of my writing workshop, which would not have happened otherwise. Whatever your situation, take advantage of test pressure as an excuse to carve out more time for writing. We cannot let testing take the little writing time we have and transform it into canned drill sessions. Our responsibility is to help students evolve as writers and thinkers, with or without testing.

Publishing

I often wonder if students find it odd or inauthentic that, although I constantly instruct them to imagine a specific audience when writing, for most assignments I am their only audience. I do realize that the workshop lays the groundwork for students to write for one audience or another—be it a boss, a board, or a roomful of convention attendees—but I have tried to make the workshop more worldly by requiring students to attempt to publish their work in various ways. Some ideas of how I do this are on the next page.

Class Readings

In the second quarter, I have students select what they consider their best or favorite piece from the preceding quarter and read it to the class. I usually return several assignments completed at the end of the first quarter on day one of the new quarter and have students file the material in their finished folders. Thus, all students have their finished folders open and updated on their desks. From there, it is easy for them to choose an assignment to read aloud. I find this practice beneficial because students get to hear what their classmates have been doing for the past two months; they must tune their ears and mind's eye outward after the intense internal focus of the workshop. It is also good work for each student to literally give voice to his or her own words, to physically breathe life into the words so they take flight in the air of the classroom. To hear one's own words float before a group can be a nerve-wracking but powerful experience.

I have never had a student refuse to read aloud, but not all of them are excited to do it. Some select a poem from the previous quarter, since it is usually their shortest work. Whatever they choose, giving voice to their own words and listening to the words of others serves as a filling station for the new quarter, an oasis of sorts where we rest for a while from the work of writing and take a long drink.

Sending Letters

Writing various types of letters—a letter for social action, a letter to the editor, a friendly letter, and a thank-you letter—and actually mailing them, has several benefits. It creates a teachable moment about stuffing and addressing an envelope, a lost art in our current world of screens and texts. But more than that, the act of sending one's written words out into the world gives students a sense of connection and power. And it is gratifying for students when they receive responses, especially when they have sent a letter urging social action to politicians or companies. Even receiving a form letter holds some weight with students: The world has replied. Students sometimes get personal notes from political staffers or even politicians themselves. A student of mine got a phone call in response to the letter he sent to our state representative. A phone message came to the school, asking Chris to return the call. Chris, as it happened, was a budding politician himself and was positively elated. He returned the call that afternoon and had a lengthy chat with one of the representative's aides. The principal at my current school works hard each year to respond to the letters that are sent to him. Even on a smaller scale, students who receive friendly letters or thank-you notes from friends or relatives get to experience the feeling of connection that comes when someone has taken the time to write a letter and mail it. One never knows who will bite when words are cast out into the world.

On a practical note, I have experimented with different ways to provide envelopes and stamps for students. Sometimes my class budget allows it; sometimes I have to buy

Writing Workshop in Middle School © 2013 by Marilyn Pryle • Scholastic

them myself. Other times I have required students to either bring in their own stamps or purchase one from me. Your personal situation (school policies, budget, and so on) will determine what is best for your class.

In-School Publications

A good place to begin exploring printed publications is the school newspaper or literary journal. Not all middle schools have them, but maybe some particularly eager writing students would be willing to start their own publication. At any rate, I have found that students are usually excited to publish work for their peers, and their peers are even more excited to read what their classmates have written. When copies of our literary journal, *The Cougar Review*, first came hot off the photocopier, students were so excited that we had to make a rule banning the reading of the *Review* during class time unless specifically allowed by the teacher.

Cross-Curricular Idea!

- Pair writing students with art students and have them create a collaborative work for display.
- Have a music class accompany a poetry reading.

School journals and newspapers are just one way to publish in school. We schedule poetry events in April, National Poetry Month, during which we display student poetry on hall bulletin boards and select students to read their poems over the school PA after announcements. We also host literary readings once a year at the local library and invite family and friends of the students.

Depending on your school, publishing can take many forms. Work could be posted in the cafeteria; writing could be paired with artwork and displayed. A single piece of writing or two could be highlighted each week and photocopied on one sheet (thereby eliminating the need for a journal cover). Writing can be posted in the form of an online literary journal on the school's Web site. The options are abundant.

Writer's Market and *Poet's Market*

At the end of the year, I have students submit a handwritten piece of work, accompanied by a cover letter, to a print journal. I own a copy of both *Writer's Market* and *Poet's Market*, two telephone-book style guides to all that is published in the world. These can be found in any bookstore, but since they are expensive, you may want to check your local library for copies.

These books are too time-consuming for students to navigate, but I comb through them myself, type up a document with a dozen or so publishers of children's magazines or journals, and make enough copies for classroom use. Both books arrange publishers alphabetically, but there are subject indexes in the back of each. I sift through the many entries listed under "Children" in the index, first eliminating those for book publishers or contest guidelines. I sort out the magazines and journals, and then choose the most appropriate ones. Each entry gives an editor's name, the magazine's address, and the type of writing they publish. I make my selections and retype the information for students. From this handout, students must choose one magazine they think would be the best fit for the piece they want to send out. Then they compose their cover letters using the information on the handout.

Writer's Market and *Poet's Market* are published every year, but this does not mean you have to buy them every year or that you cannot use a copy that is a few years old. Most of the journals and magazines listed in the books also post the same information on their Web sites; after consulting the index for journal titles, you can verify the most current submission guidelines for each journal online.

I make the writing of a submission letter an actual assignment at the end of the year, and I teach a mini-lesson about which elements should be included in a cover letter. I save this assignment for the end because I want students to choose the single best piece from the entire year. Make sure they use their home addresses, since they may not receive a response until the end of the summer or fall.

Even though many of the magazines and journals listed in these guides accept online or e-mailed submissions, I have students submit their work in print to give them the experience of sending out their own words in hard copy and also so they get extra practice in writing and mailing letters. In addition, this is the traditional method that writers use. My goal is for students to have the experience of selecting an appropriate publisher for their work, marketing themselves in a cover letter, packaging their words, including a self-addressed stamped envelope, and hoping for a response. This hope completes the circle of writing; plus, it forces students to experience the lost art of patient anticipation!

Online Reviews

One sure way to publish is through reviews on book-related Web sites such as amazon.com. These sites accept all appropriate reviews, and students can see their writing within a few days. As time goes on, they can even monitor how many people have found their review helpful! The obvious drawback to this method is the need for an account on these sites. Perhaps you can set up a group account. Although the group name ("Ms. Pryle's Class") would be listed at the top of each review, students are free to include their own name or an abbreviation at the end of the review in order to distinguish it as theirs. Be sure to secure parental and administrative consent before doing this.

Writing Workshop in Middle School © 2013 by Marilyn Pryle • Scholastic

The World

Although sending one's work into the world may be one natural conclusion to the writing process, it is never the goal. It is difficult to create something genuine with one eye fixed on the outside world. The inner workings of the mind, alone in the moment of creation, is the gift of a writing workshop. It is the gift of being alone and undisturbed in the peace of the creative zone. Finding this gift is not necessarily easy, but the challenge it presents is also a gift. After a writer has connected with her own creative energy, then, and only then, can she meet the world in a new way and respond to it with writing that is hers and hers alone.

Chapter 10

Variations of Writing Workshop: Literature and ELL Classes

A wonderful aspect of writing workshop is that it is malleable. It can be shaped to the needs of students and teacher; it can be molded to fit into external boundaries of time and curriculum. It can be expanded or contracted, made easier or more difficult. Since the goal of writing workshop is simply to improve each student's abilities as a writer, thinker, and expresser of his or her ideas, there is no time limit on achievement. There is only good effort. As teachers, we provide a nook of space and time for students to think and to write what they think. That nook can take many forms.

In this chapter, I give some concrete ideas about how to shape the workshop to fit different scenarios in the classroom. I explore ways that bursts of writing workshop could complement a traditional literature class, and I provide helpful tips for adapting the workshop for ELL learners. Whatever your situation, I believe you'll find ways to incorporate at least some of the most important aspects of writing workshop into your classroom and have students reap the benefits of it.

Literature Class

Student Note

"Now, even when I'm reading, I'll think to myself, 'Oh, that's some nice sensory detail.'"

—*Nina L.*

Weaving writing workshop into a traditional literature class can be especially fruitful. Instead of merely reacting to literature, students get to understand literature from the inside out; they learn to think like writers as they read. I often wish I could teach a writing workshop and reading workshop together, with fewer classes but more time in each class to discuss literature from a writing standpoint. As it is, my students take an English class from other teachers, and though I try to draw parallels with that curriculum, I always feel one step removed. Teaching both together, even if one has to "make room" for the writing like dessert after a huge meal, can be extremely satisfying.

Students often approach me with examples drawn from their literature class of a specific technique that we've practiced in writing workshop. A student may discover a short story that begins with a sensory detail, or a character description that fully illustrates that character's clothing style. Students are usually proud of themselves for finding it, and I like to photocopy their examples for future use.

Writing assignments not only reinforce the concepts taught in literature class, they can also take the place of some of the instruction. Concepts such as setting, character, plot, conflict, climax, theme, rhyme scheme, and meter can all be introduced through writing assignments. You'll be teaching these ideas anyway; why not have students actually *try* them out? This way, they will actively internalize the information rather than passively taking notes and trying to memorize it.

> Incorporating writing workshop into a literature class teaches the major techniques of literature from the inside out.

Where to Start: Choosing Genre Assignments

Refer to the goals for writing workshop you brainstormed in Chapter 2. What are your goals? Do you want to use writing only to reinforce literary concepts in narration and poetry, or should your students be able to write persuasively as well? Usually the answer is both. One path to achieving both goals appears below (see pages 145–151 of the Appendix for a description of these assignments):

Genre Assignments to Complement a Literature Class
Setting Sketch
Character Sketch
Autobiographical Incident
Free Verse Poem
Analysis of a Short Story
Analysis of a Poem
Short Story
Poem in Form
Book Review
Compare-and-Contrast Essay
Personal Essay

We start the year with a focus on setting and character sketches, enabling students to begin with familiar subject matter and laying a foundation for them to understand these two critical components of literature. All year, you can refer back to the details and development of setting and characterization you established in these assignments. In addition, since students have generated and chosen the details themselves, you can reiterate throughout the year the idea that authors select details to suit their purpose—no detail is random. Beginning the year with these two concrete, fun, nonthreatening assignments can go far in preparing students for all that they will read thereafter. Students can write before any reading they do, or they can write and read concurrently, using parts of a story or an entire story as their sample reading for the assignments.

An Autobiographical Incident assignment weaves together setting and character, and provides a scaffold for introducing plot and theme. A Free-Verse Poem assignment draws upon the concept of sensory detail covered in setting and character, and adds an opportunity to teach figurative language. Both assignments can be accompanied with sample reading from the curriculum.

Assignments on the analysis of short stories and poetry are commonplace in literature classes. As a result of your students' immersion in literature and focus on literary techniques thus far, they will be familiar with this kind of analysis and be able to perform at a deep level. From there, students can try new challenges, like writing a fictional story from scratch or writing a poem in a specific form. Both of these assignments would be difficult to do without the assignments leading up to them. Or rather, students could write them, but the finished products would not be very sophisticated. On the other hand, once students have explored the basic elements of fiction and poetry in an autobiographical framework with the first four assignments, and once they have completed in-depth analyses of well-formed works in both genres, they are ready to try writing their own fiction and formal poetry.

A Book Review assignment pushes students toward true persuasive writing. (Short story and poem analyses can also be viewed through a persuasive lens. You can teach the analyses with a more persuasive slant; however, the idea of a "claim" in an analysis is a sophisticated one and may prove difficult at that point.) To write a book review, students use what they know about analyzing literature and structure their ideas in a persuasive framework. A Compare-and-Contrast Essay assignment can also involve persuasive writing by requiring students to both analyze and synthesize works from the curriculum. Personal essays, in which students can draw from anything they read during the year to prove their theses, also involve persuasion.

Of course, this list of assignments is just one way to integrate literature and writing workshop. Other assignments, such as a ballad, legend, or historical fiction, can also be used to instruct and reinforce the literature curriculum. Your allotted time for writing may determine the number and genres you choose. Whatever your situation, teaching through authentic writing assignments in which students choose all topics and learn literary elements by writing about their own lives is most fruitful.

Mini-Lessons

The mini-lessons you teach with each assignment can be drawn mostly from your curriculum. For example, one of the most effective ways to discuss story leads is to have students examine and chart the techniques employed in the first few sentences of the stories in their readers (whether they have read the full stories yet or not). This technique can be used for examining titles or essay clinchers. When discussing strong verbs, you can isolate a paragraph from a story or essay from your classroom text and have students list all its verbs, or you could choose an entire short story and ask students to list "Words Instead of *Said*" or "Verbs for How People Move." These methods can also be applied to the teaching of sensory details. Analyzing two or three texts at a time is a way to identify different organizational patterns for stories, poems, or essays. A well-considered English curriculum and a universal reader can serve as powerful tools for budding writers. A wealth of examples exists at their fingertips; they only need to learn to view themselves as active creators of language as they read the work of others.

It's best to focus on just one mini-lesson besides the mini-lesson introducing the genre itself. Certainly, if you have time, you can teach as many mini-lessons as you want, but you should plan on choosing the most important characteristic to teach with a given genre assignment and concentrate on it.

Below is a list of mini-lessons to present after introducing the genre assignments in the list on page 135.

Craft Mini-Lessons for the Literature Workshop

Genre Assignment	Mini-Lesson
Setting Sketch	Sensory Details
Character Sketch	Introductions
Autobiographical Incident	Theme
Free Verse Poem	Simile, Onomatopoeia, or Personification
Analysis of a Short Story	Elements of a Short Story
Analysis of a Poem	Rhyme Scheme
Short Story	Ways to Start a Story
Poem in Form	Meter
Book Review	How to Develop an Opinion About Literature
Compare-and-Contrast Essay	Conclusions
Personal Essay	Crafting a Thesis

This is just one way to organize important topics. You can rearrange, combine, or add topics to suit your needs. The important thing is not to overwhelm yourself or your students by trying to teach everything with every assignment. It's too much, it takes too long, and it kills the momentum and energy of a piece. As I have emphasized, once a concept is taught, it should be applied to every subsequent assignment. So, for example, once students understand and practice the idea of theme in their autobiographical incidents, they are expected to continue creating and finding themes in the rest of the year's assignments.

Finding the Time

A regular English class does not afford the luxury of having days and days to cover a variety of mini-lessons, let students write at their own pace in class, and conference with each student multiple times over one piece of writing. The whole process must be condensed, and much of it will be done at home. Based on past experience, I suggest the following procedure:

1. **Spend a class introducing the assignment, looking at some sample reading with students, teaching one mini-lesson, and getting students started on prewriting.**

Remember that if you read or refer to the existing curriculum as your sample reading, this first class will overlap with curriculum work. This is doubly true if you use something from your curriculum in your craft mini-lesson. This type of mini-lesson would be taught on a second and even a third day within a full-time writing workshop. Within the limited time frame of an English class, these two lessons could be taught back-to-back. Or, if you have the time, you could save the craft mini-lesson for the following day, using just a portion of that day's class.

It is important to have students begin (or even finish) their prewriting in class while the instruction and examples are fresh in their minds. A solid prewriting will ensure a better quality of writing at home, where students will write their drafts.

2. **Assign the drafting portion of the assignment for homework.**

You can give students two or three days, or a week—whatever you feel is appropriate for their level and the assignment itself—to complete a draft. I require students to type a draft, write on it in colored pen or pencil so I can see their revisions, and then type and print a revised copy. You can also send students home with an Editing/Revising Checklist to complete and incorporate into their drafts. When the due date arrives, have students hand in their drafts and prewriting together, so the entire assignment stays intact.

3. **Read, revise, and correct students' writing at home.**

This is appropriate in a full-time workshop as well. Make sure to correct in a way that does not spell out exactly what you're looking for, but only indicates the need for a change. Choose one focus point that you want to discuss with the student and make a note to yourself on the student's paper. If appropriate, write a note to the student explaining an aspect he or she could work on.

4. Set a day aside for in-class revising and conferencing.

This would be a true workshop day, where students revise their papers based on your written suggestions while you circulate throughout the room helping them. Due to time constraints, check in briefly with students to see how they're doing and help individuals with one aspect of their piece. You won't be able to cover everything with each student, but students will be able to figure much out on their own. Remember that students gain a lot when they improve in just one area, even if the rest of the piece is not perfect. Go easy on yourself and do your best.

5. Give students one or two nights at home to implement the new revisions and then collect and grade them.

You may have to edit your rubric to grade so it relates only to what you taught in class and what you expect from your students' revisions, which is fine. You may also want to give students another chance to revise—not with in-class time but at home. You can also try to meet a student who is struggling after school or during other free time.

If needed, you can trim this process even more, by introducing the assignment in half of a class, assigning sample reading and prewriting for homework that night, and assigning the drafts for the following nights. I recommend holding on to the workshop day at all costs, but if need be, even the revisions can be relegated to homework (although you would need to give students at least one additional chance to revise before awarding a final grade, since they would be trying to figure out your notes about correcting and revising on their own). Do whatever you can, and don't get discouraged! Preserve the most important aspects:

> **Do What You Can!**
>
> Even if almost all the work you give is homework, you can still preserve the following:
>
> 1. Real genres
> 2. Choice of topic
> 3. Emphasis on process
> 4. Grade improvement through revision

- Students write in real genres.
- Students choose their own topics.
- You emphasize process and revising.
- Students can better their grades through meaningful revision.

The more class time and teacher availability the better, but these four principles can be upheld while students do the bulk of the work at home.

FINDING TIME: SOME VARIATIONS ON WRITING WORKSHOP

	SOME CLASS TIME AVAILABLE	LESS CLASS TIME AVAILABLE	NO CLASS TIME AVAILABLE

STEP 1	One entire class period:
	• Introduce assignment
	• Read samples together
	• Teach one mini-lesson
	• Begin prewriting
	• Homework:
	  ◊ Finish prewriting
		Half of a class period:
		• Introduce assignment
		• Read samples
		• Homework:
		  ◊ Prewriting
			Homework:
			◊ Read Assignment Sheet directions
			◊ Read samples
			◊ Prewriting

STEP 2	Part of a class period:
	• Check prewriting
	• Answer questions
	• Homework:
	  ◊ Draft/Revision (give 2+ nights)
		Part of a class period:
		• Check prewriting
		• Answer questions
		• Homework:
		  ◊ Draft/Revision (give 2 + nights)
			Following class:
			• Answer questions
			Homework:
			◊ Draft/Revision (give 2+ nights)

STEP 3	One entire class period:
	• Return graded papers; students revise
	• Circulate and answer questions
	• Homework:
	  ◊ Finish revision/reprint new final
		Part of a class period:
		• Return graded papers
		• Show 2–3 common revisions on projector
		• Homework:
		  ◊ Finish revision/reprint new final
			• Homework:
			  ◊ Take graded paper home and revise
			  ◊ Print revision and bring to class
			• Let students revise again if needed; address most common revisions with whole class

Writing Workshop in Middle School © 2013 by Marilyn Pryle • Scholastic

ELL Classes

Although English Language Learners can complete most of the assignments listed in Chapter 2, the method and scope of teaching the genres will differ. ELLs obviously need more guidance and intervention during a writing workshop, whereas native English-speaking students can work for days on their own. For ELLs, I must repeatedly explain steps, directions, and vocabulary. Likewise, ELLs require that I spend more time on mini-lessons, and they often need to learn basic computer skills as simple as using the tab key or selecting double-space from the set-up menu. Writing workshop with ELL students also differs from a traditional one because it involves more listening and speaking in the prewriting stage. This important step grounds students in the writing assignment, generates vocabulary, and helps them organize their ideas.

How an ELL Writing Workshop Differs From Typical Writing Workshops

- ELLs need more explanation of steps, vocabulary, sample reading, and mini-lessons.
- ELLs need additional help with computer skills.
- ELLs require more listening/speaking exercises.
- Teacher needs to model all steps of the writing process for every assignment.
- Revision must be explicitly and repeatedly taught.

After the first assignment or two, I typically give students only the finished product to read as a model; with ELLs, it is important to constantly model all steps to the writing process. This is beneficial on many levels. First, most native-speaking elementary school students are familiar with a brainstorming list or web, but many ELLs are not. Moreover, a filled-out sample prewriting sheet can present many useful new vocabulary words, some of which students may want to use in their own assignment. In addition to the finished sample essays, I usually do my own version of each writing exercise and copy my brainstorming, drafts and final paper onto overheads for the students to see.

ELL Teaching Tip

Complete each writing activity yourself and save all your prewriting and drafts. Show these to students (via overhead or handout) so they can see the writing process. You can also model specific vocabulary, conventions, sentence structures, and organizational patterns.

Showing ELL students models of drafts in the revision process is vital at the beginning of the writing workshop. Many students who have not written in a workshop setting do not even understand the meaning of the word *draft*, even when it is explained repeatedly. This is a cultural difference, in many cases; students think the goal is to hand in finished, "perfect" papers the first time. In the past, when I've instructed students to mark up their drafts with a pen, some are reluctant to do so; they want to use Wite-Out so no "mistakes" show. Therefore, giving students a sample of a draft covered with crossed-out lines, notes, respellings, arrows, circles, and so on helps them see what I expect them to do. Often I hand these sample drafts out as photocopies, but it is also particularly effective to mark up a draft on an overhead so students can witness the revisions as they're being made. Showing a sample paper-in-revision also presents an opportunity to demonstrate common grammar, spelling, or organizational errors.

For my ELL classes, I run more of a semi-workshop—although students write on their own, and I visit them individually for conferencing, they receive much more guidance and full-class teaching during the prewriting stage. Additionally, my ELLs, when finished with a writing activity, do not continue to the next assignment on their own as in a typical writing workshop. The ELL class starts each assignment together.

ELL Classes and Grading

With ELLs, I sometimes downplay grades. Depending on the level of the student, when I read a paper for the first time, I may not write down any numbers at all. I don't want the student to become discouraged if he or she is struggling, and I don't want the student to feel that every mark made on paper is going to be graded. Sometimes I even detach the rubric from the bottom of the assignment sheet and clip it to the assignment when the writing is well on its way. Of course, it's up to teachers to judge whether students need the motivation of the visible rubric or if the thought of being graded will be too discouraging.

With ELL papers, I often grade based on one or two grammatical topics and let the rest go. For English teachers, letting certain areas go unchecked can be difficult, but for some students the experience of seeing all their errors marked is daunting. Focusing on patterns allows the student to practice and internalize one or two concepts at a time.

Grammar Mini-Lessons

Certain genre assignments have a way of lending themselves to teachable moments in grammar. When teaching a Setting Sketch assignment to ELL students, one might also teach prepositions related to place; during a Character Sketch assignment, the focus could be on the third-person present tense. An Autobiographical Incident assignment provides a forum for the past perfect tense. In addition to dealing individually with ELLs through student conferences, a whole-class mini-lesson that focuses on one grammatical point can also be beneficial.

Writing Workshop in Middle School © 2013 by Marilyn Pryle • Scholastic

Small-Group Listening and Speaking Activities

As any ELL teacher knows, the four components of language learning (reading, writing, listening, and speaking) are best learned in conjunction with one another, not in isolation. Group activities are designed to help students understand each genre, generate vocabulary for the writing assignment, and/or provide practice on some of the spotlighted conventions for the assignment. In addition, the benefits students get from simply interacting with each other and trying to communicate are immeasurable: each student brings a variety of experience and knowledge to the group. For example, when talking about sensory details and preparing students to write a Setting Sketch assignment, I usually do one or two of the following partner or group activities:

- **Sensory Details Scavenger Hunt:** Give pairs of students lists of about twenty sensory detail words, such as *red, smooth, tall, salty, square*, and so on, and take them to a place (or make the words applicable to the classroom) where they can search for objects to match the details. When pairs have found objects for each detail, they can take turns sharing their findings with the rest of the class.

- **Draw a Picture:** Students draw a picture of a place, then pair up and describe their picture to a partner. In order to encourage discussion, the listening partner must think of two questions to ask the describing partner about the place. Then, together, they can generate lists of vocabulary words related to the places they drew.

- **5 Senses Game:** Place an object (e.g., an old shoe) or a picture of something (e.g., a crowded street) in the middle of a group of two to five students. Write each of the five senses (or draw a nose, eye, hand, tongue, and ear) on a separate index card; repeat this three more times for a total of twenty cards. Place the cards in the middle of the group, and have students take turns drawing a card and offering a corresponding sensory detail for the object or picture. After all twenty cards have been drawn, shuffle and repeat with a new object or picture.

- **Re-create a Space:** This is one of my favorite partner activities for practicing prepositions. Draw a basic diagram of a place (e.g., an open side view of a house, an aerial view of a room or a park, a map of a town) without any details. Include only entrances, walls, or basic landmarks. Distribute a diagram to each student and then pair students. Give Partner A a list of ten items—furniture, plants, and so on—to draw anywhere on his or her picture, without showing Partner B. When finished, Partner A must describe the position of the added items, relative to the original drawing, using sentences such as, "A sofa is on the wall next to the front door." Partner B can ask questions but may not view Partner A's diagram. Partner B draws all of the items based on Partner A's descriptions, then the partners compare their diagrams for accuracy. The wonderful Pair Work series by Peter Watcyn-Jones has several of these activities already prepared for photocopying.

Taking the time to have students talk and share ideas before writing boosts their confidence, multiplies their ideas, and increases their understanding of the task.

Whatever the level of the ELL class, it has been my experience that students benefit from writing about their own lives and thoughts, no matter how brief or jumbled the attempt. ELLs must practice using English in a meaningful, personal way if they are to incorporate it into their lives.

*   *   *

Certainly, a wide variety of writing workshops exists to suit the parameters and needs of just about any classroom. Whatever your situation, never become discouraged over a lack of time or resources, slow student progress, or pressures from testing or curriculum. Your intent to guide students in a genuine and meaningful way toward clearer and deeper self-expression contributes immensely to their lives and to the world. Your belief in the value of writing helps our students and our schools. As we tell students, trust in the process. The rest will follow.

Easy Genre Assignments

GENRE ASSIGNMENT	DESCRIPTION	FITTING MINI-LESSONS	GRADE 7 CCSS
Autobiographical Essay	A true account taken from the student's life, focusing on sensory detail, setting, characters, and theme	Sensory Details, Theme, Introductions: Narrative, Quoting Dialogue, Words Instead of "Said," Ways to End Narrative	W.7.3–7.6, 7.10
Character Sketch	An autobiographical description of a family member or friend using the touchstones of what the person looks like, does, and says	Elements of Characterization (Looks, Says, Does), Using Sensory Details, Theme, Quoting Dialogue	W.7.3.a–d, 7.4–6, 7.10
Classification Essay	An essay that breaks down a topic into smaller, labeled parts, focusing on paragraph formation	Brainstorming/ Grouping, Webbing, Transition Words, Introductions: Essays	W.7.2, 7.4–7.6, 7–10
Descriptive Essay	An essay describing a topic, focusing on sensory detail	Sensory Details, Transition Words, Introductions: Essays	W.7.2, 7.4–7.6, 7.10
Eyewitness Account	A third-person essay detailing an event, focusing on sensory detail and chronological order	Sensory Details, Chronological Organization, Transition Words	W.7.3–7.6, 7.10
Free Choice	Any genre assignment on this list; good for extra work or the end of the semester or year	Mini-lessons will vary.	W.7.4–7.6, 7.10
Free-Verse Poem	A poem without a rhyme scheme or meter, focusing on detail, theme, similes, onomatopoeia, alliteration, and/or personification	Sensory Details, Theme, Similes, Onomatopoeia, Alliteration, Personification, Line Breaks	W.7.4–7.6, 7.10 L.7.5*

continued on next page

Easy Genre Assignments, continued

Introductory Letter	A letter introducing the writer (student) to the reader (teacher or class), focusing on organizing paragraphs	Brainstorming/ Grouping, How to Set up a Letter	W.7.2–7.6, 7.10
Memo	A short note focusing on one or two main points	Audience Awareness, Tone	W.7.2, 7.4–7.6, 7.10
Newspaper Account	A short third-person report detailing the who, what, when, where, and why of an event	5 Ws of a Newspaper Article	W.7.2–7.6, 7.10
Ode	A free-verse poem in praise of something, employing sensory detail, similes, onomatopoeia, and so on	Sensory Details, Theme, Similes, Onomatopoeia Alliteration, Personification, Line Breaks	W.7.4–7.6, 7.10 L.7.5*
Process Essay	A how-to essay explaining a process step by step	Sequential Organization, Transition Words, Introductions: Essays	W.7.2–7.6, 7.10
Setting Sketch	An autobiographical description of a familiar place, focusing on sensory details	Sensory Detail, Brainstorming/ Grouping	W.7.2–7.6, 7.10
Thank-You Letter	A note or letter of gratitude, to be mailed	How to Set up a Letter, Tone, Audience Awareness	W.7.2–7.6, 7.10

* Since the CCSS do not address writing poetry, I have correlated language standards to this assignment.

Intermediate Genre Assignments

GENRE ASSIGNMENT	DESCRIPTION	FITTING MINI-LESSONS	GRADE 7 CCSS
Analysis of a Short Story	An in-depth study of a short story focusing on characters, setting, plot, theme, and symbolism	Parts of a Short Story (can be separated), Organizing an Analysis, Quoting a Source, Summarizing	W.7.2–7.6, 7.9.a, 7.10
Ballad	A narrative poem (rhyming/meter optional) employing sensory detail, plot, and possibly a refrain	Using Rhyme, Using Meter, Sensory Details	W.7.3–7.6, 7.10; L.7.5*
Business Letter	A letter of inquiry, praise, or complaint to a business, to be mailed	Organizing a Business Letter, Addressing an Envelope, Audience Awareness, Tone	W.7.2–7.6, 7.10
Children's Book	A basic children's story employing characters, setting, plot, and theme; can be illustrated and bound	Elements of Characterization, Sensory Detail, Theme, Using Rhyme, Using Meter	W.7.3–7.6, 7.10
Compare/Contrast Essay	An essay that compares and contrasts two topics, focusing on organization of paragraphs and persuasion in the conclusion	Venn diagram, Two Ways of Organizing Compare/Contrast, Transition Words, Conclusions, Introductions: Essays	W.7.2, 7.4–7.6, 7.10
Letter for Social Change	A persuasive letter written to an appropriate political or social agent, to be mailed	Topics for Social Change, How to Set up a Letter, Persuasive Clinchers, Tone, Audience Awareness	W.7.1, 7.4–7.6, 7.10
Letter of Submission for Publication	A letter to a book publisher requesting publication of an enclosed story, poem, or essay	The Literary Outside World, How to Set up a Letter, Tone, Audience Awareness	W.7.2, 7.4–7.6, 7.10

continued on next page

Intermediate Genre Assignments, continued

Persuasive Essay	An essay stating and supporting an opinion	Fact versus Opinion, Persuasive Topics, Organizing Persuasion, Introductions: Essays, Persuasive Clinchers	W.7.1, 7.4–7.6, 7.8, 7.10
Reflection Paper	An organized reflection on a reading or other work	How to Reflect on Literature, How to Quote Fiction, How to Quote Poetry, Introductions: Essays	W.7.1, 7.4–7.6, 7.9, 7.10
Résumé	A list of accomplishments and experience	Tone, Audience Awareness, Keeping Consistent Tense	W.7.4–7.6, 7.10
Retelling of a Legend	A rewriting of a legend (cultural or family), using characterization and setting	Sensory Details, Introductions: Narrative, Words Instead of *Said*, Ways to End a Narrative	W.7.3–7.6, 7.8, 7.10
Short Story	A narrative with developed characters, setting, plot, and theme	Parts of a Short Story (can be separated), Introductions: Narrative, Choosing a Narrative Voice, Character Motivation, Mood	W.7.3–7.6, 7.10
Test Writing With Prompt	An essay or narrative in response to a sample standardized test prompt	Mini-lessons will vary, but can include prewriting techniques (brainstorming/ grouping, webbing), Test-Taking Tips	W.7.1–7.6, 7.10
Travel Brochure	A description of a familiar place with a persuasive slant; can be printed as a brochure	Sensory Detail, Organizing Persuasion, Introductions: Essays, Persuasive Clinchers	W.7.2, 7.4–7.6, 7.8, 7.10

* *Since the CCSS do not address writing poetry, I have correlated language standards to this assignment.*

Advanced Genre Assignments

GENRE ASSIGNMENT	DESCRIPTION	FITTING MINI-LESSONS	GRADE 7 CCSS
Analysis of a Poem	An in-depth study of one poem highlighting concepts including rhyme, meter, imagery, symbolism, alliteration, line breaks, theme, and sensory detail	Rhyme Scheme, Mapping Meter, Organizing an Analysis, How to Quote a Poem, Linking Form and Content in Poetry	W.7.2, 7.4–7.6, 7.9.b, 7.10 L.7.5*
Article From an Interview	An essay written after a live interview, including an introduction, short biography/ background, excerpts, and conclusion	Creating Interview Questions, Organizing an Interview	W.7.2, 7.4–7.6, 7–10
Arts Review	An opinion essay about a CD, movie, television show, or visual artwork	How to Quote a Song, How to Develop an Opinion About the Arts, Creating a Thesis, Introductions: Essays, Conclusions	W.7.1, 7.4–7.6, 7.8, 7.10
Book Review	An opinion essay about an entire book	Elements of a Book Review, How to Develop an Opinion about Literature, Creating a Thesis	W.7.1, 7.4–7.6, 7.9.a, 7.10
Cover Letter for a Résumé/ Application	A letter introducing the writer and his/ her training, experience, and interests	How to Set up a Letter, Addressing an Envelope, Audience Awareness, Tone	W.7.2, 7.4–7.6, 7.10

continued on next page

Advanced Genre Assignments, continued

Drama	A short play focusing on character, setting, plot, and theme	Elements of Characterization, Theme, Setting up a Script, Stage Directions	W.7.3–7.6, 7.10
Historical Fiction	A short story, complete with developed characters, setting, plot, and theme, based on an actual time or event in history; some research necessary	Choosing a Narrative Voice, Character Motivation, Researching History, Introductions: Narrative, Ways to End Narrative	W.7.3–7.10
Longer Fiction/ Novel Beginning	A beginning of a longer story with developed (or planned) characters, setting, plot, and theme	Choosing a Narrative Voice, Character Motivation	W.7.3–7.6, 7.10
Parody	A satirical rewriting of a poem or story, focusing (and twisting) the style or meaning of the original	Goals in Parody, Tone	W.7.4–7.6, 7.9, 7.10
Personal Essay	A meditation on a certain topic (e.g., love, popularity, baseball, being a teenager) incorporating autobiography, research, and literature	Creating a Thesis, How to Use a Quotation Dictionary, Summarizing, Introductions: Essays	W.7.1–7.10
Research Paper	A longer paper with a thesis supported by research	Organizing a Research Paper, Creating a Thesis, Conducting Research, Quoting a Source, Paraphrasing, Citing a Source, Works Cited	W.7.1, 7.4–7.8, 7.10

continued on next page

Advanced Genre Assignments, continued

Rhyming Poem	A poem employing a rhyme scheme (meter optional)	Sensory Details, Using Rhyme, Similes, Onomatopoeia, Alliteration, Using Meter	W.7.4–7.6, 7.10 L.7.5*
Science Fiction	A short story, complete with developed characters, setting, plot, and theme, employing scientific aspects; some research necessary	Choosing a Narrative Voice, Character Motivation, Researching Science, Introductions: Narrative, Ways to End Narrative	W.7.3–7.8, 7.10
Various Poems in Form	A formal poem, such as a sonnet, sestina, or villanelle	Using Rhyme, Using Meter, Linking Form and Content in Poetry	W.7.4–7.6, 7.10 L.7.5*

* Since the CCSS do not address writing poetry, I have correlated language standards to this assignment.

Creating a Yearly Curriculum

Complete this planning page for each quarter.

QUARTER _____

POSSIBLE GENRE ASSIGNMENTS	POSSIBLE MINI-LESSONS

Editing/Revising Checklist 1

Read your draft. Then answer the questions below to help you revise.

	YES	NEED TO REVISE
1. Do I have an introduction?		
2. Does each paragraph contain **one main idea** with examples?		
3. Do I have a conclusion?		
4. Do I **avoid** banned words such as *good, bad, cool, stuff,* and *things*?		
5. Do I avoid clichés?		
6. Do I **try** to use transition words like *however, although, moreover, consequently,* and *in addition to*?		
7. Did I use the spell-checker?		
8. Did I check all commas? (Should they be periods?)		
9. Did I capitalize all proper names and titles?		

Editing/Revising Checklist 2

Read your draft. Use the questions below to help you revise.

1. What kind of introduction do I have? (*Circle one.*)

    Question   *Imagine . . .*   *Interesting fact*   *Quote*

    Sensory detail (sight, sound, smell, taste, touch)

    Other (describe) _____

2. What is in my conclusion? (*Circle any that apply.*)

    Summary of ideas   *Theme or message*   *Solution to a problem*

    Opinion   *Frame with introduction*

    Other (describe) _____

3. Do I use any banned words or clichés? If so, replace them. What is one banned word I use often? _____

4. Do I include at least three transition words? _____

5. Do I use weak verbs? If so, replace some. _____

6. Are my sentences varied? Are they different lengths with different beginnings?

    _____

7. Find one flat sentence and change it.

8. Did I use the spell-checker? _____

9. Did I look up any unfamiliar homophones? _____ Name one: _____

10. Check all commas. Should I change any to periods? _____

11. What is one special problem I should check for in my writing? (Write it below and check for it.)

    _____

Editing/Revising Checklist 3

Read your draft. Use the questions below to help you revise.

1. What technique did I use for my introduction? _____

2. What technique did I use for my conclusion? _____

3. How is my organization? Describe it: _____

   _____

4. Language: Banned words? _____   Weak verbs? _____

5. Do I have sentence variation? _____ Transition words? _____

6. What is my tone for this piece? _____

   Is it appropriate for my audience? _____

7. Did I use the spell-checker? _____

8. Are all my verbs in the same tense? _____

9. What is one punctuation rule I should check for? Check for it.

   _____

10. What are two problems I should check for in my writing?

    • _____

    • _____

    Check for them.

Editing/Revising Checklist 4

Read your draft. Use the questions below to help you revise.

Structure and Organization: List three areas you should always check, and check them:

Areas   Checked

1. _____   ☐

2. _____   ☐

3. _____   ☐

Description and Language: List three areas and check them:

Areas   Checked

1. _____   ☐

2. _____   ☐

3. _____   ☐

Grammar and Spelling: List three areas and check them:

Areas   Checked

1. _____   ☐

2. _____   ☐

3. _____   ☐

Special Problems: List two problem areas that you have been working on this year:

Areas   Checked

1. _____   ☐

2. _____   ☐

Assignment Log

Name _____ School Year _____

#	DATE	ASSIGNMENT NAME (GENRE)	TITLE

Sample Conference Record Chart

CLASS:

M	T	W	Th	F			M	T	W	Th	F			M	T	W	Th	F			M	T	W	Th	F

M	T	W	Th	F			M	T	W	Th	F			M	T	W	Th	F			M	T	W	Th	F

M	T	W	Th	F			M	T	W	Th	F			M	T	W	Th	F			M	T	W	Th	F

M	T	W	Th	F			M	T	W	Th	F			M	T	W	Th	F			M	T	W	Th	F

M	T	W	Th	F			M	T	W	Th	F			M	T	W	Th	F			M	T	W	Th	F

M	T	W	Th	F			M	T	W	Th	F			M	T	W	Th	F			M	T	W	Th	F

Name _____ Date _____ Class _____

Writing Survey

1. What kind of writing do you do on any given day?

☐ School note-taking   ☐ Academic essays   ☐ Blog

☐ Notes to a friend   ☐ Homework exercises ☐ Letters

☐ Shopping lists   ☐ Online reviews   ☐ Journal/Diary

☐ To-do lists   ☐ Work-related writing (for a job)

☐ Texts   ☐ Creative writing (stories, poems, plays)

☐ E-mail

☐ Social network posts ☐ Other _____

Answer the following questions on a separate sheet of paper. Explain your answers fully.

2. In your opinion, what makes someone a good writer? List at least three things.

3. What kinds of writing in school (essays, stories, poems, research papers) are you best at? Why?

4. What kinds of writing in school do you struggle with? Why?

5. What was the best piece of writing you ever wrote? When did you write it? Why do you think it was your best?

6. When you are writing, what is the easiest part for you (thinking of ideas, planning, getting started, using examples, writing an ending, and so on)? Explain.

7. When you are writing, what is the most challenging part for you (thinking of ideas, planning, getting started, elaborating, writing an ending, and so on)? Explain.

8. How do you plan out what you are going to write? What is the difference between when you plan out your writing and when you don't?

9. When you write for school, do you leave everything until the last minute? How does that affect your writing?

9a. Do you ever revise your writing? What do you do when you revise?

10. What would you like to learn this year about writing?

End-of-the-Year Writing Survey

Look through everything you've written in your final writing folder as you think about the questions below. Look also at your writing survey from the beginning of the year. Answer the questions on a separate sheet of paper and explain your answers fully.

1. What was the most enjoyable assignment to write this year? Why?

2. What was the easiest assignment for you to write? Why?

3. What was the most difficult assignment for you? Why?

4. Aside from your answer to #3, what assignment did you least like writing? Why?

5. How would you describe "the writing process" to someone? What does it mean to you?

6. Did you enjoy revising everything you wrote this year? Why or why not? Do you think it helped you?

7. Reread your writing survey from the beginning of the year. Has anything changed? Explain.

8. What do you think it takes to be a good writer?

9. What was your favorite part of the class? What aspect of the class (big or small) seemed to help you the most?

10. In writing all of the assignments this year, what did you learn about yourself as a person?